Splitting the
DMAIC

D1218591

Also available from ASQ Quality Press:

The Certified Six Sigma Green Belt Handbook, Second Edition
Roderick A. Munro, Govindarajan Ramu, and Daniel J. Zrymiak

The ASQ Six Sigma Black Belt Pocket Guide
T.M. Kubiak

The Certified Six Sigma Black Belt Handbook, Third Edition
T.M. Kubiak and Donald W. Benbow

The ASQ CSSBB Study Guide
Mark Allen Durivage and Shawn Findlater

Statistics for Six Sigma Black Belts
Matthew A. Barsalou

The ASQ CSSGB Study Guide
Roderick A. Munro, Daniel J. Zrymiak, and Elizabeth J. Rice

The Certified Six Sigma Yellow Belt Handbook
Govindarajan Ramu

Six Sigma Green Belt, Round 2: Making Your Next Project Better than the Last One
Tracy L. Owens

The ASQ CSSYB Study Guide
Erica L. Farmer and Grace L. Duffy

The ASQ CQE Study Guide
Connie M. Borror and Sarah E. Burke

The Probability Workbook
Mary McShane-Vaughn

The Certified Quality Engineer Handbook, Fourth Edition
Sarah E. Burke and Rachel T. Silvestrini, editor

The Quality Toolbox, Second Edition
Nancy R. Tague

The Certified Manager of Quality/Organizational Excellence Handbook, Fourth Edition
Russell T. Westcott, editor

To request a complimentary catalog of ASQ Quality Press publications, call 800-248-1946, or visit our Web site at http://www.asq.org/quality-press.

Splitting the DMAIC

Unleashing the Power of Continuous Improvement

Tom Quick

ASQ Quality Press
Milwaukee, Wisconsin

American Society for Quality, Quality Press, Milwaukee, WI 53203
© 2019 by ASQ.
All rights reserved. Published 2019.
Printed in the United States of America.

24 23 22 21 20 19   5 4 3 2 1

Library of Congress Cataloging-in-Publication Data
Names: Quick, Tom, 1961- author.
Title: Splitting the DMAIC: unleashing the power of continuous improvement /
    Tom Quick.
Other titles: Splitting the define-measure-analyze-improve-control
Description: Milwaukee, WI : American Society for Quality, Quality Press,
    [2018] | Includes bibliographical references.
Identifiers: LCCN 2018050767 (print) | LCCN 2018051808 (ebook) |
    ISBN 9780873899796 (softcover: alk. paper)
Subjects: LCSH: Production management. | Continuous improvement process. |
    Organizational effectiveness. | Six sigma (Quality control standard)
Classification: LCC TS155 (ebook) | LCC TS155 .Q48 2018 (print) |
    DDC 658.5—dc23
LC record available at https://lccn.loc.gov/2018050767

No part of this book may be reproduced in any form or by any means, electronic,
mechanical, photocopying, recording, or otherwise, without the prior written
permission of the publisher.

Director, Quality Press and Programs: Ray Zielke
Managing Editor: Paul Daniel O'Mara
Sr. Creative Services Specialist: Randy L. Benson

ASQ Mission: The American Society for Quality advances individual,
organizational, and community excellence worldwide through learning,
quality improvement, and knowledge exchange.

Attention Bookstores, Wholesalers, Schools, and Corporations: ASQ Quality
Press books, video, audio, and software are available at quantity discounts with
bulk purchases for business, educational, or instructional use. For information,
please contact ASQ Quality Press at 800-248-1946, or write to ASQ Quality Press,
P.O. Box 3005, Milwaukee, WI 53201-3005.

To place orders or to request ASQ membership information, call 800-248-1946.
Visit our Web site at www.asq.org/quality-press.

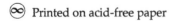 Printed on acid-free paper

Quality Press
600 N. Plankinton Ave.
Milwaukee, WI 53203-2914
E-mail: authors@asq.org

ASQ **The Global Voice of Quality®**

Dedication

I'm lucky to have met great people who have mentored and inspired me throughout my career. This book is dedicated to them—Mike Wilson, Michael Gelb, Tracy Owens (aka Rainmaker), and Eric Lavelle (rest in peace.)

And to Lisa, my true life partner, without whom there would be no meaning.

* * *

Contents

* * *

List of Figures and Tables

* * *

Foreword

In *Splitting the DMAIC,* Tom Quick does a great job of providing organizations with a simple, practical approach to problem solving. I am confident that his concepts of ensuring you start with quality katas and focusing on actions rather than tools will provide a clear roadmap for your team's success.

Tom is spot on with his interpretation of companies becoming too enticed with having a few green or black belts on the team to drive continuous improvement. He points out that their emphasis should be on matching the right people with the right training to solve the right problems. *Splitting the DMAIC* gets to the heart of why so many organizations fail to move the needle after implementing and investing into Lean Six Sigma programs.

William J. Walton III
COO Metal North America
Ardagh Group

* * *

Preface

Does any of this sound familiar?

A large company has had a Lean Six Sigma effort going for five or six years. The exact start date isn't clear because the effort began in one plant where a new plant manager who happened to have some skills from a previous company led a very successful project that eliminated a nagging defect and greatly reduced the costs associated with handling the defect. Since other plants had the same defect, the effort was deemed a "best practice" and all other plants had to now implement "lean six sigma" projects.

Some of the plants tried. One appointed the EHS manager to also handle LSS because he had some yellow belt training in the past. Another gave it to the assistant engineering manager, who wasn't really working out in his current role anyway. Others just renamed their usual fire-fighting efforts as LSS projects. Everyone claimed wins in the monthly calls, but there was little evidence in the numbers.

After a year or so, the company decided they needed more training to be successful, so they put someone from corporate HR in charge and she promptly hired a consulting company that specialized in "belt" training. They decided there would be yellow belts, green belts, and black belts. Yellow belts would get one day of training to become familiar with concepts and learn the vocabulary. Green belts would get two weeks of training and be required to complete a project. Black belts got the same training as green belts but had to complete two projects instead of one with a higher expected value. No one would be certified until the projects were complete, the steps audited to make sure something hadn't been skipped, and the "savings" verified by a controller.

Over the next couple years, many were trained. Each plant was asked to volunteer two or three people. Those chosen to volunteer were usually the quality manager or an assistant manager and/or one of the newer process engineers. One plant even discovered they had a former black belt in their midst and sent him. The training was very professional and covered all of the LSS tools anyone could possibly need. It explained the DMAIC methodology, where each tool fit into each step, and how some tools could be used in multiple steps. People enjoyed the training but complained that it covered too much material in the time allowed. At times, it felt like they were trying to drink from a firehose. Still, they were eager to try out their new skills and returned to their plants with a lot of enthusiasm.

After a while, it was noticed that even though a lot of people had been trained, very few had been "certified." Most projects just seemed to peter out somewhere in "A" or "I" phase. People had trouble finding the time to work on their projects and do their full-time jobs. Attendance by other team members was low for the same reasons. One crisis or another would take priority over the project.

Project selection was also a problem. The trainees were expected to come up with their own projects and even though the plants had many problems, appropriate projects were difficult to identify. It was hard to figure out the "savings" from potential projects in order to meet the certification requirements. A lot of projects didn't seem to align with the plant's priorities and so got little support. The chosen projects ended up being either the most difficult issue a plant was facing—some years in the making—or simply a capital project that had already been planned.

Naturally, there were some successes, and these were heralded as examples of how to do it right. But the successes were difficult to duplicate in other locations. It also seemed as though there were only a few people who could get it right and finish a project. Success seemed to depend on the skill of the leader even though everyone had the same training.

So, after years of effort in time and money, here is where they found themselves:

- A lot of people with training but no skills

- A lot of projects started but not finished

- A lot of projects finished with little impact

- A lot of frustration and skepticism about Lean Six Sigma

Sound at all familiar?

If so, you might be one of the frustrated people out there who have bought into the promise but can't seem to deliver. You've done everything you've been told to do, but somehow still have a low percentage of wins. Maybe you blame yourself, or your training materials, or your hiring process.

The truth is none of that. The problem is not with you or your people or your methods. The problem is with the approach. The problem is in the way we go about continuous improvement.

There must be a better way!

There is!!

* * *

Introduction

Why do a company's continuous improvement efforts fail to deliver expectations or reach potential impact?

There is no doubt that the various improvement methods work. Whether it is PDCA or 7-Step problem-solving or A3 or Is–Is Not or DMAIC or any other tool, it has been used to great success in many organizations stretching back over decades. (PDCA was introduced by Shewhart in 1920.)

Why have some been successful and others not?

Could it be that those organizations had better people with better skills? Perhaps the key was a charismatic leader who inspired success? Or maybe they just had to make it work in order to survive—the proverbial burning platform? If any of these were the true reason, then all would be lost to the fates. Organizations without some lucky hiring, or a visionary, or the right combination of market forces could never make CI successful. (To make it simple, I'll refer to all of the various methodologies—LSS, PDCA, DMAIC, and others—as continuous improvement, or CI.)

Fortunately, the answer is something accessible to all. Anyone, anywhere, can make CI work by following this one simple trick—er, sorry, too much internet. Anyone, anywhere, can make CI work by "splitting the DMAIC." Let's explore what that means.

Introduction

Splitting the DMAIC

Much of today's CI training is focused on tools. The training includes days or even weeks working through every possible tool a practitioner of CI might need. (The lists illustrated in Figures 1 and 2 are typical.) The tool is presented along with its various iterations and the potential timing of its use (many tools can be used in several steps).

The Lean Six Sigma Process...

D M A I C

Define	Measure	Analyze	Improve	Control
VoC / VoP	MSA (GR&R)	7 Wastes	Brainstorming	SPC
SIPOC	Process Map	Pareto	DoE	Audit
CTQ Tree	Process Capability	ANOVA	RSM	Poke Yoke
SWOT	Sampling	Hypothesis Testing	Pull / Kanban	RACI
QFD	DILO	Correlation	Pugh Matrix	Management System
CoPQ	OEE	Regression	Piloting	Kaizen Team
Kano Model	VSM	FMEA	SMED	Control Plan
Stakeholder Analysis	RTY	5 Whys	...	Tolerancing
Project Charter	...	Ishikawa		...
...		Transfer Function		
		Benchmarking		
		...		

Figure 1 Example of DMAIC complexity.

Figure 2 Another example of DMAIC complexity.

Some trainers delight in covering the rare and obscure ways a tool can be used...because you never know. Then there are the contrived examples that bear little resemblance to what the poor student will face in real life.

Sometimes people are asked to bring projects with them to training so they can work on "actual" problems. The training then forces them to apply tools that don't make any sense, so they can "learn." Someone working on downtime is forced to evaluate whether the durations reported by the computers are correct, as if measurement of elapsed time is a mysterious and difficult thing. Everyone must do a value-stream map and calculate Takt time even if it has nothing to do with the problem they are working on.

These new trainees are then sent back to their worlds to try to figure out how to navigate through the DMAIC methodology, choose the appropriate tools to use, and make some sort of improvement. It's kind of like teaching someone how a wrench works and then expecting them to repair a machine. Sure, some are successful, but they tend to be the exception. How can we increase the success rate?

As it turns out, when you examine a lot of successful projects, you find that there are a few common paths through the DMAIC and that these paths are used repeatedly. These common paths have similar objectives and share a common set of tools.

The most common paths through the DMAIC relate to following objectives:

- Reduce variability of a characteristic

- Reduce failures of a machine

- Reduce waste in a process

- Reduce the frequency of a defect

Rather than teach people about a set of tools that they might or might not use, why not teach them how to accomplish a specific objective? Why not give them a path for solving a particular type of problem that works most of the time? Wouldn't this approach be easier and allow more people to be successful?

The rest of this book goes through each of these objectives and shows typical paths through the DMAIC. There is some discussion of the tools on the path, but most of the description and explanation of the tools is left out; many other authors cover these well. This book is more focused on when and how to use a specific tool to accomplish a specific thing. In fact, there are a couple new tools in here that were created just for the purpose where they appear!

This book also covers project selection and team management. The choice of projects is crucial to creating context and therefore success. No trainees (or teams) should choose their own project, ever! The specific goal of the effort should be determined by management and linked to objectives and metrics.

Working in teams and doing DMAIC projects is not easy. People need support and lots of help. There should clear systems that provide this support at various steps in the process. We'll look at what some of those support systems might be.

I hope this take on continuous improvement ignites your efforts and unleashes the true power of DMAIC throughout your organization.

HOW TO READ THIS BOOK

If you are like me, you often want to understand the heart of topic before diving into the details. When I'm convinced of a good idea, I want to get started right away and I have little patience for fluff and filler. Here is some advice on what to skip, or at least where to start, depending on your current role.

If you are a CEO...

I recommend you first jump to the "What Comes Next..." section (page 71) and then just skim through the descriptions of each path. This will give you all the information you need to get started with a CI approach that really works. You can always go back and fill in some of the details as needed to insure the correct approach.

If you are a Quality exec...

I would start from the beginning and work to understand each path. Sorry, but you need to fundamentally understand all the paths and be able to determine which are appropriate for your needs. This is probably the most important contribution you can make to the organization. Too many have given in to the lure, to the siren song, of LSS without truly understanding which parts apply to their business. Do the analysis required to figure out which of the paths are relevant to your situation. Then move on to execution and begin applying the appropriate methodology.

If you are a person who just wants to improve something...

Read through the path descriptions, find the one that seems to fit, and try to implement it. Ignore all the extraneous pressures and details and just focus on the steps on the path. You will be successful, and people won't care if you colored a bit outside of the lines to do it. They tend to leave successful people alone!

If you are already a black belt...

Please excuse the insinuation that you've done something wrong. Chances are you are trying to follow what you've been trained to do with all good intentions. Recognize that it's difficult to do certain things, and be willing to regroup and try again.

So, turn to the chapter that resonates most closely to your objective and try to realign to the suggested path. Not only will it make more sense to you and your team, but your chance of success will increase greatly.

Then go back and try out another path and then another. Pretty soon you will have mastered the paths.

* * *

Brief History of CI

In the following paragraphs, I will show that the basic concepts of improvement have been around for a long time. We have obfuscated simple truths by trying to combine improvement efforts into some grand universal methodology called Lean Six Sigma.

The origins of Lean Six Sigma (LSS) are not found in the 1980s when the practices of Six Sigma and Lean were merged. In fact, the start of LSS traces back to the development of statistical methods in the 1700s. In 1733, Abraham de Moivre, with Pierre-Simon Laplace, developed statistical concepts including probability and the normal curve.

These concepts were used by Eli Whitney near the end of the eighteenth century to mass produce muskets. Whitney needed to produce 10,000 muskets for the United States military and was able to accomplish this by using objective part measures. Using objective part measures allowed Whitney to create interchangeable parts that were similar enough in fit and function and that allowed for random selection of needed parts for mass assembly. This practice may seem commonplace today; however, during that period of history it was a paradigm-shifting concept. The levers that allowed for this paradigm shift were the statistical concepts developed earlier in that century. By assessing the parts in a quantifiable manner, Whitney was able to compare measurements against product specifications and determine variance from specification. Parts with too great a variation could then be excluded from the process, allowing for faster production and better quality.

Whitney had ushered in the use of quantifiable measures and analysis to improve a system and reduce waste. This essentially became the LSS platform.

As manufacturers began using quantifiable measures and analyses to improve processes and thus products, theories on how to best manage such a system began to arise. One theory that provided a strong foundation for LSS was described in *Principles of Scientific Management,* written by Frederick Winslow Taylor in 1911. This theory outlines how to manage a manufacturing process using scientific methods. Taylor found that four guiding principles were necessary to instilling and maintaining scientific management. The four principles are:

1. Replace rule of thumb with scientific process.

2. Objectively select, train, teach, and develop the workforce.

3. Cooperate to ensure all work is being done according to process.

4. Divide work equally between management and workforce.

Looking at these a little deeper, we can see that the first principle aims to reduce process variation by creating a standardized process. The second principle takes the standardized process and brings it to the workforce. The third principle calls for adherence to the standard process to ensure that no more "rules of thumb" are introduced into the process. Lastly, work should be delegated equally between those performing work and those supporting work functions. These principles provide a stable, consistent process with an adept workforce in an environment that drives improvement.

Taylor provided examples of how scientific management improved processes. In one such example, Frank and Mary Gilbreth used modern technology to improve bricklaying efficiency. The Gilbreths filmed brick-layers and performed a motion and time analysis. Using these quanti-fiable measures, they determined that raising the brick platform would decrease movement and improve efficiency. The work Taylor and the Gilbreths did in the early 1900s created the foundational concepts of the Lean Six Sigma we have today.

In the 1920s, Walter Shewhart was a factory employee who sorted waste into four categories: assignable, chance, special, and common. Assignable and chance were found to be the most frequent categories. Using statistics and standardized processes, Shewhart aimed to control a process enough to ensure that the only waste source would be chance. To achieve this goal, Shewhart developed the Plan-Do-Check-Act cycle to assess sources of waste, determine solutions, evaluate solution success, and ensure sustainability of the improved process.

What we now call Lean was really started by Henry Ford in the early 1900s. The now-famous Toyota Production System can be seen as extension of Ford's principles of "one-piece flow" and complexity reduction. Shingo built on these further with his methods for improving changeovers.

From these foundational pieces—statistical analyses, scientific management, and a standardized platform for process improvement—Six Sigma and Lean practices were born. If you look closely at the origins, you can see that the methods sprang from the need to solve a specific problem. There was not a methodology looking for a problem to solve. We seem to have it backward today; we teach methods and then go looking for problems. The need should drive the method, just as form follows function. We should get back to this. We should identify problems and then apply a method rather than teach a method and search for an application. Hopefully, you will this book a useful guide to do just that.

***

The Paths

Have you ever been in a forest and walked along a natural path? Sure, we all have. Ever stop to think where the path came from? Perhaps animals chose that way to get to their food or water. Or maybe someone went first and just forged a way through and others followed. Whatever the beginning, those traveling after found it easier to follow the same way. The path wasn't designed by an engineer or a part of some master plan. It may not be the shortest or straightest way from point A to point B and it may meander in a seemingly random way. Even so, because it is well worn by others, it must work! Those who stick to the path rarely get lost and usually end up where they are going.

DMAIC is our forest. And just like the real forest, there are a few well-worn paths created by the many others who have come before.

Standing at the entrance to our forest, it's hard to see the paths and determine where they might lead. This is what makes DMAIC so difficult and frustrating for many. Some won't even enter because the DMAIC forest is too intimidating. Some refuse to go in without an experienced guide. Others march right into the forest without knowing there are existing paths and waste time wandering around, hoping to find the right way out.

Because of this, far too few people in organizations are using this powerful methodology and fewer yet are successful. How can we eliminate much of the frustration and difficulty? How can we make DMAIC accessible to more people? How can we reduce the need for experts in order to be successful?

Let's make it easy to get through the DMAIC process! Let's make it so anyone can do it!!

Imagine if we could somehow get above the DMAIC forest, high enough to see the most common paths. What would we see? We would see a vast network of trails and paths with seeming unending complexity. These are the paths others have traveled. Some of the paths are short, ending nowhere. Some fork endlessly. Some even go in circles. But if we

9

looked closely, we would see that four paths reach from one end of the forest to the other and appear wider, smoother, and less treacherous than the others. Let's see where those paths go!

The first DMAIC path leads to *variability reduction.*

This path is used by people who want to reduce the variability around target of a desirable characteristic. Variability exists in all processes and reducing it should be a never-ending goal. For some reason, not many people have been using this path in recent years. Maybe because it seems harder than other paths? This path takes us past MSA Point, through Special Cause Canyon, and to the Plains of Control and Capability.

The next path comes out at *failure reduction.*

We are talking here about machine failures and this path generally leads to increases in throughput. Throughput is lost any time a process is not producing at its maximum potential. Understanding the sources of these losses is the purpose of this path that winds its way around Maintenance Mountain, Bottleneck Bay, and MTBF Falls.

The third path is *waste reduction.*

This is the newest path and it's very popular lately because it seems to be the easiest. However, sand pits along this path can slow down or trap the unwary who try to use it to get to the other outcomes. When followed correctly, this path leads to the fertile banks of the Value Stream, crosses the Spaghetti Swamp, and ascends Inventory Incline. For some reason, this path is also the cleanest, because travelers tend to shine and sort along the way!

The fourth path is *defect reduction.*

Defects are things that are not supposed to be there in the first place and should be eliminated. There is no target or optimal level for these other than zero. This is probably the widest, most common path and it takes us through places like Fishbone Lake and Pareto Park. Many of the tools found on this path are simple and easy to use.

These four paths are obviously not the only ways through the DMAIC forest, but they are the most common.

If we know ahead of time where we want to come out—the goal of our effort—we can know which path to take and which tools we are likely to need. This makes it easier for anyone to participate, makes it easier to train people, and reduces the need for facilitation; we need fewer "experts." Adopting these paths can give the power of improvement to a lot more people.

Now, some of the experts may not like this approach because it reduces their influence. Some don't want these methods to be clearer. They obfuscate on purpose, making things more difficult than necessary due to some twisted sense of job security or superiority. But thankfully, most of our current experts would be thrilled to expand the base of users and actually see more improvements faster. Think of what could be if you double or triple the number of effective problem-solvers in your organization.

Splitting the DMAIC by using the paths can make it so! Let's take a closer look at each one.

Here is how the discussion of each path is organized. For each path, the following will be presented:

- Methodology—an overview of the purpose and actual steps through the DMAIC process for that path.

- Step Details—a detailed description of each step including specific tools used. In some steps you will find new tools you have not seen before. Yes, you are allowed to make up your own tools!

- Checklist—a simple one-page sheet that anyone can use as a guide along the path. Think of these as a new app called DMAIC Maps, which helps people get around the DMAIC world the same way Google Maps helps in the real world.

* * *

Reducing Variability Path

This path is used to improve the control and capability of an output characteristic. Here the word *control* means achieving a stable and predictable process and *capability* means the output is reliably within specifications. Yes, it's the SS in LSS! A lot of people can explain, and some even correctly, what six sigma quality is supposed to mean. Everyone has seen a picture of a normal distribution with percentages labeled to four decimal points and arrows pointing the slivers way out on the tails. That's Six Sigma! Alas, few people know how to actually get there anymore.

Whatever happened to statistical quality control (SQC/SPC)? It used to be all the rage before Lean came along and sucked up all of the CI air. Control charting was the first thing I learned as a budding quality guy in the mid-1980s. (I remember creating a charting program using Symphony macros!) When is the last time you saw it as a topic at a conference? Sure, you find control chart construction explained in green belt training, but that's far from SPC. (In fact, as I'll explain in a bit, one of the key failings of SPC efforts is starting with the control chart. You'll see below that it doesn't show up on my path until step 7!) It's a little like teaching a Gantt chart and expecting people will know how to do project management. We confuse a tool with a methodology.

SPC was once the cornerstone of any respectable quality program. Where did it go? Perhaps it became old-school? Or perhaps it was too hard?

Or maybe there was just no clear strategy for getting a particular characteristic under control. Until now!

In my travels, I've seen a lot of SPC efforts fail. Usually started with great fanfare, the charts are put in place and the expectation is for immediate, amazing results. Of course this doesn't happen, so "SPC doesn't work."

But if you examine the failures, you find a number of key reasons:

- The process inputs weren't well-understood.
- The sampling mixed up sources of variability.
- The charts weren't set up right.
- There was no thought to a reaction plan.

Or perhaps it was all of the above, and maybe a few other reasons as well.

This specific set of steps, a path if you will, was created to avoid these key reasons for failure. It has been used all over the world in many different types of processes with great success. It is easy to teach and follow. It has proven to be very robust and I know it can work for you.

METHODOLOGY

Here are the steps that are effective at reducing variability:

1. Process map
2. Input/output matrix
3. Specifications and targets
4. SOPs
5. Measurement
6. Set-up and potential analysis
7. Control and capability analysis
8. Handle special causes
9. Reduce common causes
10. Capture learnings

STEP DETAILS

To understand the steps in this path it is important to keep in mind the basic concepts of statistical management as articulated by ASQ's Statistics Division a long time ago. These are:

- Everything is a process.
- All processes have variation.
- All decisions recognize variability.
- Reducing variability improves quality.

To understand how these concepts apply, consider that quality control really boils down to just two steps:

1. Collect some sort of data.

2. Decide whether to do something.

Both steps are fraught with risk, but let's focus on the decision step. Too often, that decision is made by comparing the collected results to a specification. This leads to either reacting too late, which is a problem for the customer, or reacting too often, which is a problem for production. One leads to higher defects, the other leads to higher variability.

The only proper way to make the decision is by using statistical limits. Doing so ensures you only react when there has been an actual shift in the process. I'll not go into SPC theory any farther than this, but it's critical that people at least understand this much. Success on this path depends on it.

Let's now look at the steps.

1. Process Map

The first four steps on this path are designed to capture the current knowledge about a process. We start with a process map. The purpose of the process map is to visually display when and where all inputs enter the process. The process map is a combination of a flow chart and a SIPOC model (Figure 3).

To do:

1. Start with a detailed flowchart of the process.

2. Identify the inputs and outputs for each step in the flowchart.

3. Identify suppliers and customers.

You will end up with something that looks like this for a coating process (Figure 4).

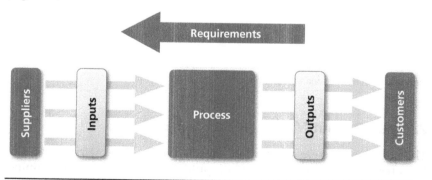

Figure 3 SIPOC model.

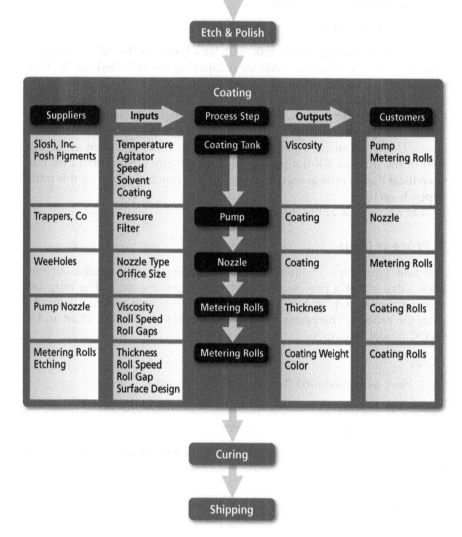

Figure 4 Process map for a coating process.

2. Input/Output Matrix

The next step is to create an input/output matrix. This matrix shows the links between process inputs and outputs and it is a key tool for gaining process understanding. It's always surprising and rewarding to watch various process experts discuss/argue about which inputs are really important and which outputs they affect. The resulting picture helps everyone's understanding and forms the foundation of setup procedures, control plans, and engineering logs. It can also highlight where there are gaps in process knowledge.

To Do:

1. List the inputs from the process map down the left side of the matrix.

2. List the outputs across the top of the matrix.

3. Some things will appear as both an input and an output; that's OK.

4. Determine which inputs affect which outputs by rating the relationships as either:

   • critical (or strong or high),

   • moderate (or weak or low), or

   • none.

5. Put a symbol or letter in the matrix that signifies the relationship.

You'll end up with something similar to the matrix illustrated in Figure 5.

3. Specifications and Targets

The next step in capturing current knowledge of the process is to collect or determine the specifications and targets for each critical input. This step is the most important. The idea is to describe what "perfect" looks like at each step in the process map. Eventually, these targets will describe the very best way to run a process. Some people refer to these as centerlines.

To Do:

1. Transfer critical inputs from input/output matrix.

2. Classify critical inputs into types:

   • fixed (has a target setting that should be maintained at all times),

   • adjustable (has target setting that may be changed during normal operation), or

   • uncontrollable (cannot currently adjust, but has an affect).

3. Determine targets and upper and lower limits for each input.

Inputs	Viscosity	Solids	Volume	Thickness	Weight	Fade	Color
			Outputs				
Temperature	High		High	High	High		
Agitator Speed	High						
Solvent	High	High		High	High		
Coating	High	High	High	High	High		High
Filter			High		High		
Pressure			High				
Nozzle Type			High	High	Low		
Orifice Size			High	High	High		
Viscosity				High	High	Low	Low
MR Speed				High	High		
MR Gap				High	High		
MR Thickness					Low		
CR Speed					High		
CR Gap					High		
Surface Finish					Low		
Design					Low		

Relationship ● High ⊖ Low

Figure 5 Input/output matrix.

4. Standard Operating Procedures (SOPs)

Operating procedures must be standardized—everyone doing things the same way—to be of any value. The biggest benefit from SOPs comes when they are developed, so as many process owners as possible should be involved.

The key types of procedures for any process are these:

- Setup
- Measurement
- Operation
- Reaction

Use the targets and specs chart to help determine which SOPs are needed for each key operation. For example, setup SOPs should address all fixed inputs and operation and reaction SOPs should explain all adjustable inputs. Operation or reaction plans should cover how to handle the uncontrollable things that every process faces.

Review and train everyone involved in the use of all SOPs. Training is very important and must be done well. The One Point Lesson (OPL) format is a great way to create and train SOPs. SOPs should be the law! But people can't follow the law if they don't know about or don't understand it. Ways must be found to make sure everyone knows when changes or improvements are made to SOPs. An SOP for SOPs can insure that all procedures are well developed and deployed.

It is likely that there will be gaps between the procedures you have and those that are needed. Plans should be made to close these gaps, but bear in mind that details in the procedures will likely change once control begins. This is where the new learning happens and SOPs are our best way to capture and transfer new knowledge.

5. Measurement

Although this step is considered to be in the "M" phase, it is actually often the first improvement step. Measurement is often a significant contributor to the observed variability in a process. Improving measurement, in and of itself, can result in better process results. In the worst case, your process could actually be perfect, but you adjust and react anyway because of differences in measurement!

Most green belts are familiar with an R&R study, but there are actually four parts to a proper analysis of a measurement system. They are:

- R&R (repeatability and reproducibility)
- Discrimination
- Capability
- Stability

You can sometimes get the analysis of the first three with the same set of data, but let's talk about them separately so we can be clear on the purpose of each.

R&R

The purpose of this study is to determine whether different people get different results using the same gauges. They shouldn't!

To do this, several people measure the same parts or standards several times. (I'll not cover the details of the calculations because they are covered well in other texts. For a good reference on Measurement System Analysis, see *Six Sigma Green Belt, Round 2,* by Tracy Owens.) The main thing is that when we see differences, action is required:

- Train or retrain people

- Rewrite SOPs

- Change gauge

Note that it also possible to assess accuracy if a known standard is included as one (or all) of the samples. Then, if there are differences between people, you'll know who is right. If people differences cannot be eliminated, then measurement should be limited to only those who can be certified to get the right results. In fact, it is a good idea to maintain a list of certified people on every gauge.

Discrimination

The next question we answer when evaluating a measurement system is whether the gauge can used to make adjustment decisions. That is, can the gauge tell when a process has shifted and reaction is required? This decision, of course, is critical to process control.

A measurement process is said to discriminate if the "normal" variability in the process can be divided into sufficient distinct categories. A sufficient number of categories is usually defined as a minimum of five, but this varies.

The problem is that sample selection has a huge influence on this result. Samples taken from the extremes will result in better discrimination than samples taken at random.

I prefer to define a meaningful shift that we wish to detect and then determine whether the measurement variability is below that.

Here is the general procedure:

- Choose 25 samples from the process.

- Measure each three times.

- Calculate measurement variability.

- Compare to size of critical shift or desired detection level.

Note that some use the results from the R&R study to determine discrimination. This is fine as long as samples are chosen wisely.

One interesting thing to do is to plot this data on a control chart (Figure 6). It will be one of the few times you want the mean chart to be wildly out-of-control! This indicates discrimination.

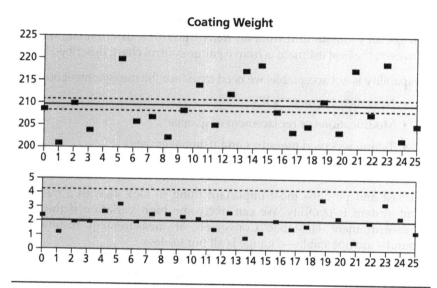

Figure 6 Control chart indicating discrimination.

If a gauge fails discrimination, then measurement variability must be reduced before the gauge can be used for process control. This can be done in one of two ways:

- By increasing resolution.
- By measuring the same thing multiple times and using averages.
- Or by improving the gauge.

Capability

The other decision we make from measurements is whether production is OK to ship. To make this decision, the measurement system must be capable of dividing the specification width into sufficient intervals. Again, a sufficient number of intervals is usually a minimum of five with 10 or more preferred. If measurement variability results in only one or two intervals between specifications, it will be difficult to say whether the output is truly in or out of specification. And the odds of making the wrong decision are high. Often, it's the customer who lets us know we made the wrong decision by complaining. Of course, our QC records will say that everything was OK! If you face complaints from your customers that you can't verify, you may want to look at the capability of your measurements.

Capability is usually expressed by the P/T (precision-to-tolerance) ratio. It is simply the width of the measurement variability divided by the spec width.

Measurement variability can be determined a number of ways. You get an estimate of it from an R&R study or a discrimination study. However, the best estimate is from a gauge control chart, described below.

If capability is not acceptable, we need to reduce the measurement error by:

- New measurement SOPs
- Modifications or replacement of gauges
- Taking repeated measures and using averages

Stability

The last and perhaps most important thing to look at with a measurement system is stability. We can overcome high variation if the mean of measurement is stable. Conversely, if measurement results drift around—are not stable—a gauge is all but useless.

To measure stability, we simply set up a control chart for the gauge by measuring the same set of samples over and over again. For this to work, the measurement system cannot be destructive in any way. In this case, destructive means that the act of measuring changes the mean value. This is not a trivial concern and should be verified to be the case. Many seemingly innocent measures actually change the value of what is being measured. Traceable standards are ideal for this kind of study.

The measurement error calculated from this control chart is the best estimate of true gauge variability.

Once a control chart has been established, it can be used at any time to determine the status of the gauge. If there is a signal from the process, an issue from the gauge can easily be ruled out as a cause. In fact, as long as the control chart shows stability, there is no need to maintain or recalibrate. Believe it or not, sometimes recalibration is a special cause source of an apparent shift in the process.

6. Setup-and-Potential Analysis

The next step is to determine the very best a process can be by performing a setup-and-potential analysis. This analysis will test how well our initial input targets and setup procedures work. If a process is not capable of producing under the best of conditions, it doesn't have a prayer of being capable when exposed to long-term influences.

The first time through all input settings and SOPs should be verified. We should pretend that we are looking at a process that we have never seen before. Some of the input targets may be estimates and many of the SOPs may be new to us. This may require tearing a machine down to check some basic alignments, gaps, angles, and loads.

To perform the study:

- Verify that all fixed inputs are on target.
- Set adjustable inputs to initial values.
- Initiate process logs and record current values of all inputs.
- Run process at design speed.
- Collect and measure 30 to 50 samples.

We can then analyze the data and determine whether the process is potentially capable. First, look at a histogram of the data (Figure 7):

- Is the observed distribution what was expected?
- Is there evidence of multiple processes?

If something looks unusual, investigate and try to explain. Repeat the study if necessary.

Next, calculate the capability indices Cp and Cpk (Matthew A. Barsalou. *Statistics for Six Sigma Black Belt*. ASQ, Milwaukee, WI. 2014.) and ask:

- Is the process on target? (The easiest way to see this is if Cpk = Cp. This indicates the process is centered.)
- Is the process potentially capable (Cpk > 1.3)?

If the process is off target and/or capability is not acceptable, react and repeat.

If the process is not capable once on target, then process control is even more important. It is the only way to minimize the amount of output that will be out of specification.

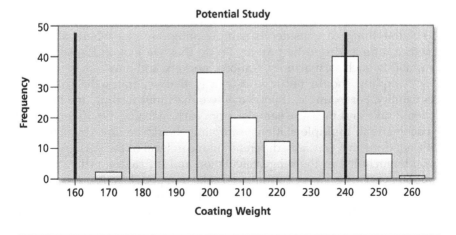

Figure 7   Histogram with evidence of multiple processes (Bimodal).

You also have to face the fact that this process has never been capable and produces out-of-spec results all the time. Are you currently sorting? If not and the output is accepted by your customers, the specifications themselves may be arbitrarily too tight.

Either way, it's time to finally introduce the control chart.

7. Control and Capability Analysis

The purpose of this step is to find the natural limits of the process. We do this by "controlling" the process. That is, by reacting or adjusting only when a special cause is present and leaving the process alone otherwise.

This is where the real learning happens, where we begin to gain some fundamental understanding of what does and does not affect the process. Commitment to learning is crucial for success.

We also learn how capable the process truly is.

Short-term Study

The main purpose of the short-term study is to set up the control charts for the long-term (ongoing) study. The short-term study gives us information about:

- Sample subgrouping
- Distribution of data
- Sampling frequency
- Common cause variability (control limits)

This step is important because control charts must be constructed correctly in order for them to be effective.

Subgrouping

The first thing to consider is sample subgrouping—where and how to take samples from the process. To do this, we look at the sources of variability, such as: machines, stations/pockets, and lines.

Sampling should be done in a way that separates the sources of variability. For example, if you have two machines feeding one line, you should take and measure samples from each machine. Or, if you have a machine with multiple stations, sampling should be done by station. If it's not done this way, any difference in mean level of the various sources will be included in the range calculation and inflate the estimate of the variability. This is a very common mistake that people make.

Sometimes it is not possible to collect samples from every source during operation. In this case, care must be taken during the set-up procedure to align the sources to the same mean level.

Sometimes an additional source of variability exists within a sample. For example, measuring in a different spot might give a different result. This within-sample variability must be measured and charted separately. It is not the same as variability through time. A good control-charting software will offer a "3D" option, which allows you to look at both within- and between-sample variability.

Remember, the goal is to develop a control strategy that will tell us when the process has changed. The reaction might be very different for "within" variability shifts when compared to "between" variability shifts.

Sample Size

The next step is to figure out the proper sample size. For continuous data, we need four things:

- Alpha—the risk of reacting falsely (0.0027 for most control charts)
- Sigma—an estimate for the process standard deviation
- Delta—the smallest shift to detect in one sample
- Beta—the risk of missing that shift

The relationship between sigma and delta is the key to sample size. If delta is small compared to sigma, sample sizes will be large. (See Figure 8.)

Any statistical software will calculate the appropriate sample size from this data. If sample sizes are too large, we have to live with higher risk or reduce sigma.

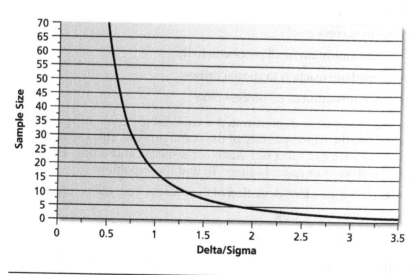

Figure 8   Sample size vs sigma shift.

Control Chart

Next we construct a control chart. Collect 25 sets of samples over a short period of time in order to limit the opportunity for any special causes to be in the data. Then calculate the appropriate statistics for each sample and plot on charts.

Sampling Frequency

The last step in the short-term study is to evaluate the control chart to determine sampling frequency. Sampling frequency is also a question of risk:

- How long are we willing to run with a shifted process?
- How likely is the process to shift in that time?

Examine the short-term charts for stability. Are they stable? If not, about how long were they stable? Are there assignable causes?

Clearly, the more stable the process, the longer we can wait between samples. Sampling frequency can be dynamic, increasing or decreasing as we gain experience.

We are now ready to begin actively controlling the process.

Transfer the control limits from the short-term study to long-term charts. Activate SOPs for:

- Sampling
- Collecting process log data
- Reaction plans

The keys to success are:

- Communication of all process activity
- Immediate reaction to special causes
- Documentation of all process data

Once the process has demonstrated a reasonable degree of stability, we can calculate the true capability of the stable process. This capability tells us how well we can meet our customer's specifications day in and day out in the absence of special causes. To find this capability:

- Estimate standard deviation of the process from the control charts
- Calculate Cp & Cpk
- Both should 1.0 or greater

If the process is not capable, we must work to improve capability right away.

8. Handle Special Causes

Once a control chart is in place, it is critical to identify and handle special causes right away. I like to think of special causes as having a short half-life; the chance of finding the cause decreases rapidly over time. That is why any special causes should be investigated according to the reaction plan as soon as they occur. A monthly meeting to review all the special causes in the previous period has no chance of success.

Special causes can be good or bad, and all special causes are an opportunity to learn about the process. Shifts in mean level can be good if one direction is better. A low run on a range chart indicates a period of lower variability. Those are hard to find and should be captured, if possible. Investigate special causes immediately.

- Was cause identified?
- Can cause be removed/repeated?
- Does process need to be adjusted?

Recurring special causes are good candidates for an additional CI effort!

9. Reduce Common Causes

The next step is reducing the common causes, which is probably the hardest thing to do. My favorite definition of *quality* is this:
"The continual reduction of variability around appropriate targets"
Of course, this means there is always too much variability. Every process would be better with less variability. But how do you do this?
Reducing common cause variability requires changing the process. The process can be changed in a number of ways:

- Changing operating procedures
- Reducing gauge error
- Reducing variability of inputs
- Reducing effect of inputs on outputs
- Eliminating or changing inputs

The number of common causes of variability is usually large and their individual effects small. Nonetheless, there may be one or two sources of variability that are larger than the rest. Finding these will take a bit of detective work and a lot of data. Thorough documentation of the process is crucial, including:

- Accurate and complete process map
- Up-to-date input/output matrix
- Meticulous recording of special cause reactions and process log data

Use this data to study the process with solid industrial research methodologies such as these:

- Hypothesis testing
- EVOP
- Experimental design

10. Capture Learnings

Finally, all learning should be captured in a structured and robust way. This locks in any gains and prevents backsliding.

- Update process map and input/output matrix. It's a good idea to make these controlled documents.
- Update all procedures and reaction plans.
- Enter lessons learned into company knowledge base if there is one.
- Share learnings with other similar process or locations.

The last thing to do is to determine what needs to be done next.

CHECKLIST

Table 1 Checklist for reducing variability.

	Step	Objectives/Key Activities	Done?
		Reducing Variability	
	Team Name:		
D	Team Information	**Organize the team**	
		Choose team leader, facilitator, and coach	
		Establish team ground rules	
		Develop communication plan	
	Process Map	**Visually describe the process**	
		Flowchart process	
		Identify inputs and outputs	
		Identify suppliers and customers	
	Input/Output Matrix	**Describe relationship between inputs and outputs**	
		Transfer inputs and outputs from process map	
		Determine which inputs affect which outputs	
		Rate the strength of the effects	
	Targets and Specifications	**Define ideal settings for critical inputs**	
		Transfer critical inputs from input/output matrix	
		Determine target values	
		Determine high and low limits	
		Classify each input	
	SOPs	**Develop all operating procedures needed to run process**	
		Develop and implement setup procedures	
		Develop and implement operating procedures	
		Develop and implement reaction procedures	
		Train all involved people in procedures	
M	Measurement	**Confirm that measurement systems are effective and stable**	
		List gauges for each measurement	
		Develop and implement gauging procedures	
		Perform R&R on all gauges	
		Study gauges for stability	
A	Setup and Potential	**Determine if process is on target and potentially capable**	
		Verify inputs are at target settings	
		Collect and measure samples	
		Determine distribution	
		Analyze for potential capability	
I	Control and Capability	**Determine common variability and long-term capability**	
		Determine control limits	
		Determine sampling plan	
		Chart process	
		Calculate true capability	
	Handling Special Causes	**Identify and appropriately handle special causes**	
		Use reaction plan to identify source of special causes	
		Study process to uncover unknown special causes	
		Categorize special causes	
	Reducing Common Cause	**Redesign process to reduce effect of common causes**	
		Determine critical sources of variability	
		Move PQI upstream where possible	
		Redesign process to reduce variability	
C	Capture Learnings	**Update all process documentation**	
		Update input/output matrix and targets	
		Update reaction plans	
		Determine future plans	

* * *

Reducing Failures Path

Reducing failures is a strategy that focuses on maximizing throughput. This path incorporates many of the elements of total productive manufacturing (TPM) that some of you may be familiar with. Maximizing throughput requires the balanced management of downtime (maintenance) and runtime (production), all the while maintaining impeccable quality.

Managing Downtime

In order to increase throughput, we must actually optimize downtime. There are two types of downtime—planned and unplanned. Unplanned downtime is insidious in that the effects often extend beyond just the lost production. Optimizing downtime means eliminating all unplanned downtime and using planned downtime most efficiently. Eliminating unplanned downtime may require increasing or better utilizing planned downtime.

Managing Runtime

Throughput can also be increased by understanding runtime constraints. This requires an intense focus and application of resources to the bottleneck process. Valuable energy is sometimes wasted by working on problems away from the bottleneck that have little leverage. Also, line configurations and modulation schemes do not always fully exploit the bottleneck.

Successfully implementing this methodology requires an intense discipline to do all the little things all the time, the patience of data-based decision making, the standardizing of equipment and practices, and the willingness to rethink the way our processes are operated and designed.

METHODOLOGY

This path starts with an analysis of asset utilization in order to identify throughput losses to be improved. This analysis can be skipped, of course, if the organization already knows the opportunities that exist, but organizations that don't understand the bottlenecks in their operation will benefit from this starting point. This analysis also shows the nature of the losses. This is critical because reducing losses due to a line changeover is not handled the same way as reducing losses due to machine failures, even though reducing either loss source is handled in these steps.

Here are the steps to improving throughput:

1. Identify opportunity
2. Define process
3. Describe operation
4. Analyze process
5. Eliminate breakdowns
6. Improve execution
7. Extend life
8. Wrap up

STEP DETAILS

1. Identify Opportunity

In the first step the team should perform an asset utilization loss analysis on the bottleneck to identify potential loss sources and choose what to work on. In some cases, these data already exist. The team will verify the opportunity by reviewing existing data.

Design Bottleneck

The classic definition of *bottleneck* is any process in which demand exceeds capacity. This is generally the operation within a process with lowest rated speed. Asset utilization is determined by the throughput of the design bottleneck. Other operations can become temporary bottlenecks, but only affect throughput if they impact the performance of the design bottleneck.

It can be complicated to determine the bottleneck, especially if the operations are not all in a straight line. But it's important to understand what part of the process is limiting the overall throughput. This limit is what defines the maximum possible throughput or 100% asset utilization (AU).

A quick word about a related measure called OEE, or overall equipment effectiveness. OEE is usually a subset of AU, where allowances are made for planned downtime. For example, if a plant only runs two eight-hour, shifts, OEE excludes the third shift. AU, on the other hand, considers it a loss to the maximum possible. There can also be allowances for maintenance or label changes or any other planned activity. Problems occur when games are played with these allowances to meet budgets or make performance look better. Another problem with the OEE approach is that it can remove the incentive to improve planned downtime activities, which can be a significant opportunity. It's fine to use OEE for this analysis as long as it's a real number and the allowances are well understood.

Asset utilization for a given period of time is a very simple calculation (Figure 9), where actual is the final good output during the time and potential is the maximum possible that could have been produced during the same time. This potential is determined by the maximum (should equal rated) speed of the bottleneck.

For example, if the maximum possible output was 1,000,000 units and you produced 750,000, your asset utilization was 75%. No allowance, no adjustments, just pure utilization.

Asset Utilization Loss Analysis

The asset utilization loss analysis breaks down throughput losses into components in order to understand the root cause(s) of the losses. There are three main categories of throughput losses:

1. Availability—the percent of time the bottleneck is available to be run

2. Efficiency—the percent of time the bottleneck is running at full speed when it is able to run

3. Yield—including all losses at or after the bottleneck

$$AU = \frac{Actual}{Potential} \times 100\%$$

Figure 9 Asset utilization formula.

Availability has two components:

1. Unplanned downtime—the time associated with all failures at the bottleneck

2. Planned downtime—the time allocated to idle time, holidays, maintenance, conversions, changeovers, and any other bottleneck downtime that is planned

There are two sources of efficiency losses:

1. Speed—losses due to reduced speed

2. Line flow—losses due to standby time at the bottleneck, when something upstream or downstream is preventing the bottleneck from producing at full speed

There are two primary sources of yield loss:

1. Scrap—in-process losses after the bottleneck

2. Defects—end-of-line quality losses

Putting it all together in a picture looks like this (Figure 10).

If these data already exist, great. Collect enough (say, 12 months) to get a good picture of the current situation. A waterfall chart is an effective way to display this type of data (Figure 11).

It can also be useful to chart each loss category through time—weekly or monthly—to see whether the overall waterfall results are typical or whether there was a one-time event inflating a category (Figure 12).

Once the loss picture is clear, it is time to choose a target process that contributes to the losses. This is often the bottleneck process, but need not be.

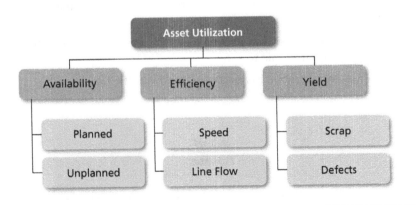

Figure 10 AU loss categories.

The team can now state a goal with respect to the losses from the target process and create an indicator to track those losses through the life of the project.

"Reduce throughput losses by decreasing discharge standby time by 25%."

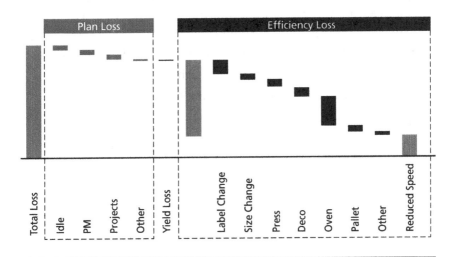

Figure 11 Waterfall chart.

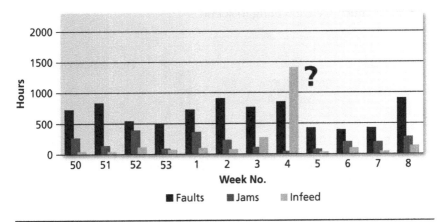

Figure 12 Weekly trend of top losses.

2. Define Target Process

Three key documents are created in the process definition step in order to define the process:

- Process flow chart
- Machine description
- Component matrix

The process flow chart (Figure 13) shows how the target machine (the one the team is working on) fits into the overall process. The process flow chart should clearly demonstrate three things:

- The relationship between the target machine and the bottleneck
- The target's infeed and discharge machines
- Buffer (accumulation) locations and relative sizes

What is a buffer?

A buffer is any accumulation of work-in-process inventory including:

- Conveying
- Balancers
- Bi-flow tables

The purpose of a buffer should be to protect the bottleneck from disruptions in line flow. The ideal size of the buffer depends on several things:

- The level of protection desired
- The risk of disruption
- How much we are willing to spend

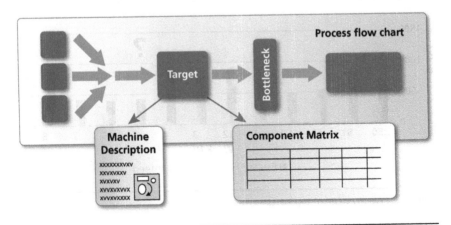

Figure 13 Process flow chart.

The level of protection provided by a buffer is determined by the length of disruption the buffer can absorb. The larger the buffer, the longer the disruption it can absorb. But buffers aren't free. The costs include:

- Initial cost
- Inventory holding costs
- Maintenance costs
- Quality costs (quality issues are usually compounded with buffers)

Now, before you Lean people jump all over me I'll acknowledge that buffers are inventory and inventory is considered a waste. I'll even agree that the long-term goal would be to eliminate buffers so they don't hide issues. But, many normal, unavoidable events make buffers essential, and they help while working on other issues. Fear not, we'll get to reducing waste, including inventory, in the next path.

The machine description document provides basic information about the target machine, including:

- Manufacturer(s)
- Model/vintage
- Serial numbers
- Upgrades/retrofits
- Rated speed

Describe any significant modifications that have been done to the machine in detail. Include a schematic that shows the basic operating principles of the major assemblies or components of the machine.

The component matrix (Figure 14) contains the information needed to improve the process. The matrix is used to gather details about:

- Components
- Failures
- Maintenance
- SOPs
- Costs

This tool was created specifically for this path. (Yes! You are allowed, even encouraged, to create your own tools. Someone has to be first.)

To create the component matrix, first develop a list of all the components in the target machine. It may be easier to first break the machine up into major assemblies and then components. You must be careful to include all components that could affect the machine's operation. Next, describe all the possible ways a component could fail. A failure is anything that ends a component's useful life or triggers a repair. Failures include wear out, breakage, loosening, product defects, and so on.

Component matrix for [target process]						
Component	Failure	PMable?	Predict	Repair?	Cost	SOP?

Figure 14   Component matrix.

Now, determine the maintainability of each failure. Maintainability indicates whether component life can be affected by maintenance.

- Positive—life can be extended, perhaps indefinitely, by preventing or reversing deterioration

- Negative—life can be shortened or deterioration accelerated by lack of activity

- None—life cannot be affected

Understanding maintainability helps focus efforts on preventive or autonomous maintenance activities that have an impact. Other methods must be used when preventive maintenance has no impact.

Next determine whether each failure is predictable. Predictable means that there is some sort of a signal that we could detect before the failure (Figure 15).

The more common failure detection methods include:

- Visual inspection

- Vibration analysis

- Oil analysis

- Thermal analysis

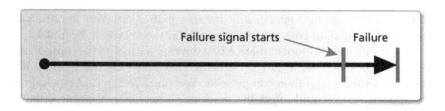

Figure 15   Component life with failure signal.

Finally, collect information about how components are repaired. For each component, ask:

- Is the component repaired or replaced?
- How much do the repair parts cost?
- Is there an SOP for this repair?

Create the component matrix including component, failure, and repair information. This component matrix will be used extensively in subsequent steps.

3. Describe Operation

The purpose of this step is to describe how the target process is operated and maintained. There are four documents to create in this step:

- Operating strategy
- Preventive maintenance
- Housekeeping
- Data collection

The team should capture actual practices in each of these documents. These documents are where the team's improvements will eventually be formalized.

The operating strategy is a description of how the plant operates the target process. The operating strategy includes:

- A statement that describes the general intention or operation of the process
- Speed settings for all run modes or how the speed is modulated, if variable
- How machines are staged, if there are multiple machines in the target process

Preventative maintenance is a document that describes all of the maintenance activities performed on the target process. The document should describe:

- Core maintenance activities by time period or cycles
- Conditional maintenance activities and the triggering signals
- Existing and needed SOPs

Compare this document with the information in the component matrix for consistency. Compare the actual maintenance activities with any known best practices and adjust, if necessary.

Conditional maintenance is maintenance that we do only when certain conditions are met. We detect these conditions in various ways:

- Visual inspections
- Quality checks
- Vibration analysis
- Oil analysis
- Component failure

It would be nice if all components gave ample warning before they failed. For each component in the process, document whether it gives a signal, how often we look for it, and how we react to that signal. Compare this information with what's in the component matrix. In particular, look for components that we said were predictable (even though we often don't look for the signal).

Housekeeping is the next document and it describes cleanliness standards and procedures for the target process. Develop and publish a cleanliness standard for the target process if one does not already exist. Photos of the desired state are helpful. Describe the current housekeeping activities. Determine whether current activities allow the standard to be consistently met. Adjust and publish new SOPs as required. Remember, cleaning provides an opportunity for inspection for signs of deterioration that should be included in the SOP.

The last document is data collection. This document describes the type, frequency, and method of data collection for the target process. The following types of data should be collected:

- Downtime causes, unplanned and planned
- Component(s) impacted
- Repairs (adjustments)
- Downtime and repair durations

Review the data collection to ensure:

- All downtime is accurately allocated
- Reason codes include all known failures
- All potential adjustments are available
- Actual planned downtime is captured

Once these documents are complete, the team is ready to begin some analysis.

4. Analyze the Process

The purpose of this step is to analyze the target process to understand the source and magnitude of throughput losses. The steps in the analysis are:

- Process performance profile
- Downtime analysis
- Runtime analysis

The process performance profile compares the minimum required performance of the target process to its actual performance. The minimum required performance is the combination of runtime and downtime that produces at least the throughput of the bottleneck. By definition, a non-bottleneck process will have excess capacity. The team needs to translate this excess capacity into an allowable loss. (Skip the process performance profile if the target process is also the bottleneck.)

Another way to think about allowable loss is to consider the buffers. The buffers, when fully ready, can absorb a certain amount of downtime at the target machine. That is the maximum length a downtime event can be without affecting the bottleneck (and therefore throughput). Events longer than this are the events of interest.

The leads us to the downtime analysis. To do this analysis, the team will need the actual duration of each downtime event, whether planned or unplanned. For unplanned events, try to collect data so that the team can break down durations into time spent on:

- Diagnosis
- Preparation
- Execution
- Setup and checkout

This will help in the improvement effort. Identify and document the root causes of the unplanned downtime events.

Next is the runtime analysis. Collect data to determine a speed profile of the target machine. A speed profile is the amount of time the target process operates at various speeds. Develop a duration distribution of reduced speed events and compare the distribution to required performance to identify the events that impact the bottleneck. The same logic used to determine maximum downtime durations can be applied to running slower speeds. How long and/or how slow can the target machine run before becoming the effective bottleneck?

Once these analyzes are complete, the identified opportunities can be prioritized for improvement.

There are three approaches to improvement. One or all of these approaches may be needed depending on the nature of the throughput losses:

- Reduce unplanned downtime by eliminating breakdowns.
- Reduce planned downtime by improving execution.
- Reduce maintenance time by extending component life.

5. Eliminate Breakdowns

The first approach deals with the unplanned downtime associated with equipment/component failures, which is the focus of this path. The goal is to remove root causes of failures and protect the bottleneck from unplanned downtime. This is done in three ways:

- Preventing failures
- Replacing a component before it fails
- Reducing repair duration

Let's look at preventing failures first.

To prevent failures, we must understand the relationship between maintainability and the life of the components that are failing. Recall that maintainability has to do with whether the life of a component can be affected by maintenance. In this context, cleaning is maintenance. We may be able to reduce failures by eliminating sources of contamination through an effective autonomous maintenance program.

For each failure event identified in the analysis, ask these questions:

- Could the failure have been prevented with maintenance?
- If so, why wasn't it prevented?
  - Are we doing the right maintenance?
  - Is the frequency appropriate?

Adjust maintenance practices and update the team's documents to reflect any changes.

If we cannot prevent failures with maintenance, we next look at replacement cycles. One sure way to prevent an unexpected breakdown is to replace a component before it fails. The replacement cycle for a given component must balance cost and risk. The ideal cycle replaces a component just before it fails. There are two ways to find the ideal cycle:

- Predictive tools
- Probability analysis

If a component gives us a signal before it fails, we can use a predictive tool to determine when to react (Figure 16).

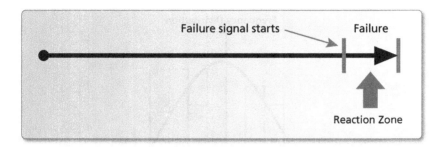

Figure 16 Opportunity for reaction.

The component matrix should contain information on the predictability of each component. Review this information for the identified failures:

- Was a predictive tool used?
- Did we get a signal?
- Did we react to the signal?
- Are we looking for the signal often enough?

The answers to these questions should drive appropriate actions. Update the component matrix as improvements are implemented

If a component does not give a failure signal, then the only way to predict failure is with a probability analysis. Probability analysis uses a frequency distribution to calculate the probability of failing in a certain amount of time. The distribution is made up of time between failures (Figure 17).

This distribution is often non-normal, so it is usually best to fit a Weibull distribution to the data. (Did you know that the family of Weibull distributions includes the normal distribution?)

We are looking for the minimum component life. That is, the amount of time during which there is a very low probability of failure. We should replace the component before this time has elapsed. Determine this minimum life from the fitted distribution and compare this life to the established replacement cycles and adjust, if necessary.

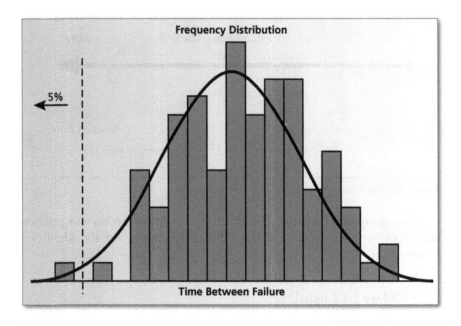

Figure 17   Distribution of times to failure.

6. Improve Execution

The next improvement area for the team has to do with reducing repair durations and planned downtime. The techniques that follow can be applied to any recurring activity or project:

- Preventative maintenance

- Changeovers

- Conversions

- Projects

The first step is to measure the amount of time currently used for each planned activity. Create a Pareto chart of planned downtime activities by duration and prioritize the activities for improvement. These may be the activities with the most potential for improvement rather than the ones with longest durations.

For each targeted activity, do the following activity analysis:

- Create a detailed list of the tasks required to compete this activity.

- Estimate the amount of time required for each task.

- Observe the activity, several times if possible, and verify task durations.
- Create a Gantt chart of the tasks.

Identify the critical path—the series of tasks that determine the overall length of the activity—and reduce the time required for these tasks. To reduce the amount of time on the critical path, look for ways to improve in:

- Preparation
  - What tasks can be done ahead of time?
  - What could go wrong?
  - Is everything needed close by?
- Execution
  - Could a quick-change assembly be used?
  - Are quick disconnects used?
  - How much motion is wasted?
- Setup/Checkout
  - How can a good setup be ensured?
  - Can adjustments be eliminated?
  - Can QA time be improved?

Those familiar with the SMED methodology (single-minute exchange of dies) will find this very similar.

7. Extend Life

The last improvement step is to lengthen the amount of time between planned maintenance activities by optimizing the primary maintenance cycle. This is perhaps the most challenging step, because it will often require redesigning components or entire machines. The techniques in this step should guide a team to improve the right things. The first step is to understand what drives the current maintenance cycle time.

Using failure and repair data, determine the limiting component in the target process and determine why it is limiting. The limiting component is the thing that requires repair the most often. It can be the component that has the shortest life and is not maintainable. Or, it is maintainable, but requires major downtime. These components are often run to failure.

You can increase the life of a limiting component by increasing the mean time between failures or by reducing the variability of the times between failure. Some ways to extend component life (mean time to failure) are:

- Lubrication
- Reduced deterioration
- Operating conditions
- Component design

You can also try to reduce the variability of component life by:

- Creating or changing SOPs
- Improving setup tolerances
- Improving vendor selection

If your actions have made an improvement, we should expect a reduction in failure rate. Failure rate improvements can be hard to determine because it usually takes a long time to collect enough data. A growth chart (Figure 18) is the fastest way to detect a change in the failure rate.

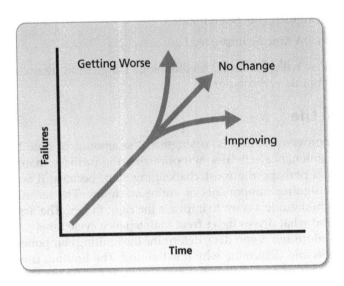

Figure 18   Growth chart.

8. Wrap Up

The purpose of this step is to capture improvements and determine next steps. This last step on the path is critical to the overall success of the team. The team's work is not finished until you have done your best to disseminate what you have learned within your plant and to all other like plants. All the team's documents should be formalized and archived.

The team should follow proper procedures for finalizing any pending SOPs and updating plant policies. Everything that the team learned should be entered into some sort of knowledge base.

The team should then formally evaluate their performance by asking these questions.

- Was the goal met?

- What was accomplished?

- How well did the team communicate?

- How could the team function better next time?

Finally, and most importantly, the team should celebrate.

CHECKLIST

Table 2   Failure reduction checklist.

		Reducing Failures	
Team Name:			
	Step	Objectives/Key Activities	Done?
D	Team Information	Organize the team	
		Choose team leader, facilitator, and coach	
		Establish team ground rules	
		Develop communication plan	
	Identify the Opportunity	Determine improvement goal	
		Perform AU loss analysis and identify loss sources	
		Determine bottleneck impact and choose target process	
		Establish indicator to measure team's success	
		Articulate goal in precise and measurable terms	
M	Define the Process	Develop a detailed definition of the target process	
		Create a Process Flow Chart of the target process	
		Develop a Machine Description	
		Develop a Component Matrix	
	Describe the Operation	Develop a detailed definition of the target process	
		Describe the Operating Strategy	
		Describe Preventative Maintenance practices	
		Describe Housekeeping standards and practices	
		Describe Data Collection procedures	
A	Analyze the Process	Determine and prioritize root causes of throughput losses	
		Create Process Performance Profile and determine allowable loss	
		Create downtime duration distribution	
		Identify events that exceed allowable downtime	
		Classify and determine root cause of downtime events	
		Perform runtime analysis for speed related losses	
I	Eliminate Breakdowns	Remove root causes of failures and eliminate bottleneck impact	
		Identify failures from analysis step	
		Re-assess maintainability information in Component Matrix	
		Confirm maintenance practices match requirements	
		Implement predictive tools to signal replacement	
		Determine ideal replacement cycles using probability analysis	
		Reduce repair durations	
	Improve Execution	Optimize the amount of time on planned downtime activities	
		Determine activities to improve	
		Perform Activity Analysis on each activity	
		Identify critical task path	
		Improve performance on critical task path	
	Extend Life	Optimize the amount of time between planned maintenance activities	
		Determine limiting components	
		Determine cause of wear out	
		Extend component life	
		Reduce component life variability	
C	Wrap Up	Capture improvements, determine next steps, and celebrate	
		Finalize SOPS, policies, team documents	
		Post lessons in Lessons Learned database	
		Evaluate team performance	
		Celebrate team's success	

* * *

Reducing Waste Path

One of the challenges I see with a lot of Belt training has to do with the way the Lean part of Lean Six Sigma is handled. Of course, Lean is a brilliant construct, and many have been very successful applying its basic ideas:

- Eliminate non-value-added activity.

- Inventory is waste.

- Production should be pulled from the customer.

Problems arise when trying to fit these ideas into the DMAIC structure. Unlike Six Sigma, which is both a philosophy and methodology, Lean is not a methodology. Much of Lean cannot be implemented by a Belt effort. Rather, what's required is a fundamental change to business structure or Lean goals are better handled as one-off improvement efforts (Kaizen events). For example, a Green belt is not able to change the production system from push to pull and is unlikely to implement one-piece flow. These require much larger efforts and technical know-how. Conversely, a Green belt could install a simple Kanban but probably wouldn't need a full-blown DMAIC project to do it.

To illustrate what I mean, here are the "key steps" for a team implementing Lean from a typical Lean website (https://kanbanize.com/lean-management/implementing-lean/):

1. Present the idea of Lean to your organization and make sure that everyone understands the change that is expected and how it will benefit the whole organization.

2. Start by separating value-adding from wasteful activities.

3. Visualize the value stream that you deliver to your customer on a Kanban board.

4. Create a smooth flow of delivering value to your customer by either alleviating or protecting the bottlenecks in your process.

5. Pull new work only when there is a demand for it and you have spare capacity.

6. Adopt the proper culture in order to achieve continuous improvement of your process.

Nice, but there is no way an ad hoc DMAIC team could actually implement these steps. Things like "...make sure that everyone understands...," "Create a smooth flow...," and "Adopt the proper culture..." are just not possible at the team level. These are enterprise level or at least plant level activities, yet many try to accomplish them with the DMAIC structure. No wonder they fail.

But there are some things a team can do well in a lean initiative if the team focuses efforts on the right paths through the DMAIC.

METHODOLOGY

So, what can a CI team reasonably do in the Lean forest?

Let's look at the types of Lean waste and how best to approach them. Using the TIMWOOD acronym, the commonly recognized Lean wastes are these:

- Transportation—the movement of things
- Inventory—especially WIP
- Motion—the movement of people
- Waiting—idle time
- Overproduction—making more than you need
- Over-processing—doing more than is needed
- Defects—scrap and spoilage

At this point in a typical LSS class, the students would be shown a few tools—value stream map, spaghetti diagram, and so on—and then told to go off and find some waste to reduce. Oh, and be sure to use all the steps in the DMAIC. Oh, and make sure the culture is aligned, too.

What are their chances for success? We can do better.

First, I strongly believe that it's up to management to determine wastes and priorities, not the student. Management has the data and visibility to understand the business impact of the various wastes and which have the biggest impact. If they don't, they have no business teaching Lean to their underlings. I've seen too often where some manager didn't get the memo saying that they were supposed to be lean, and the first they hear about it is from some hotshot "black belt." That usually doesn't go well. And nor should it! Implementing Lean principles is a strategic decision and must be driven top down. CI people should be executing specific, agreed projects arising from problems and opportunities that management has identified. (If this isn't enough of a rant for you or if you're shouting "amen" at the page and would like more ammo, go to the chapter, "What Comes Next? How You Can Do This!) Only then can we invoke the power of DMAIC teams.

Once waste-reduction targets are determined, there are specific methods that work best on each of the wastes and each has its own mini-path.

INVENTORY (AND OVERPRODUCTION)

Let's start with one of the most obvious of wastes—inventory. Almost everyone agrees that reducing inventory is a good thing. Doing so frees up cash, reduces obsolescence, and limits potential defects. But why is there inventory in the first place? It is important to understand the reason, so the proper fix can be applied. Here are some of the more common reasons for inventory:

- Seasonal demand with insufficient capacity at peak

- Inaccurate forecasting of product mix

- Poor accounting practices that reward overproduction

- Buffers to accommodate machine downtime

- General unawareness

Which of these can we expect a DMAIC effort to deal with? Really, only the last two.

Should you have enough capacity to handle peak demand? That is a strategic capital spending decision, not DMAIC. And if you did make the investment you might end up with lots of idle time in the off-peak season, which is also a waste!

Want to improve your forecast accuracy? Who doesn't? I'm not convinced it's even possible, but if a black belt could do it with DMAIC then many consultants and software companies would be out of business. Of course, eliminating the need for a forecast would be a better solution so why not build to order and not carry any inventory at all? Some have done it, but it is just not possible for many of us, especially in today's on-demand, two-day delivery economy.

OK, so how about accounting practices that create incentives to produce as much as possible in each operation in order to make machine "efficiency" look good? If you're in this situation you might be better off buying your CEO a copy of *The Goal* and forgetting any notions of implementing Lean for a while.

That leaves the last two—unplanned downtime and unawareness. Reducing unplanned downtime is the main focus of the "reduce failure" path and already has a DMAIC path that works perfectly. Reduce unplanned downtime and you can reduce the size of your in-process inventory. That leaves just awareness.

The most powerful tool for improving awareness of inventory (and thereby reducing it) is 5S. Often inventory is hard to see because it is scattered all over the place. Simply gathering like things into one place can be eye-opening. The 5S methodology is covered well in many other books, so I'll not go into those details here except to say that it's not easy! Being good at 5S requires a special, uncommon skill. (I'm terrible at it.) We should seek out those who are good it, recognize them, and maybe even certify them. Why not a 5S Black Belt? These people could then be turned loose with full support to transform the operation.

There is a reason why 5S is considered the foundation of many improvement strategies (i.e., TPM). In my opinion, it is the most powerful way to start an improvement effort. 5S involves a lot of people, has visible impact, and by itself often leads to improvements in cost, efficiency, and quality. Add to that the incredible impact on pride and morale and it's a wonder that every company everywhere hasn't already fully embraced 5S.

I've been in a lot of factories all over the world and I can sense a good 5S plant almost immediately. The people are more engaged and aware, they pay closer attention to the details, and they notice smaller deviations. This makes implementing any other improvement method easier. If your facility is not great at 5S, fix it. Become a zealot. It will be worth it.

Here is a mini-path for implementing 5S (Table 3).

If you need more details, there are a lot of good 5S resources out there for free. Or, here is a good book you can buy—*Learning Lean 5S: Quality Pocket of Knowledge (QPoK)*, ASQ, 2009.

Table 3 A 5S implementation path.

5S			
Team Name:			
	Step	Objectives/Key Activities	Done?
D	Team Information	Organize the team	
		Choose team leader, facilitator, and coach	
		Establish team ground rules	
		Develop communication plan	
	Describe the Process	Describe the process	
		Choose target process area for improvement	
		Capture current state	
		Establish timeline	
M	Sort	Separate needed and unneeded materials	
		Categorize every item in area as needed or not needed	
		Conduct "red tag" event for unsure items	
		Remove items that are not needed	

(continued)

Table 3 A 5S implementation path *(continued)*.

	Step	Objectives/Key Activities	Done?
		5S	
Team Name:			
A	Straighten	Organize work area	
		Determine which items are used most frequently	
		Determine ideal locations for items to minimize waste	
		Create marks/indicators that show where each item belongs	
I	Shine	Establish cleanliness standards	
		Perform deep clean of area to desired state	
		Determine locations for needed cleaners and cleaning equipment	
		Capture desired state with pictures/descriptions	
	Standardize	Create routines to maintain desired state	
		Detemine tasks and frequencies needed to keep desired state	
		Create schedule and assigments for tasks	
		Display record showing task completion	
		Post standards for easy comparison of current and desired states	
C	Sustain	Create systems to sustain and continuously improve	
		Create auditing system for target area	
		Publish/display audit results for target area	
		Capture needed training for 5S tasks	
		Celebrate team's success	

Kanban

Another great tool for managing inventory is the Kanban (Figure 19). Brilliant in its simplicity, the Kanban uses space and visual cues to limit the amount of inventory of a particular thing in a particular area. Use of

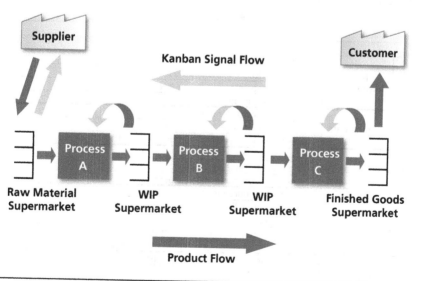

Figure 19 Kanban signal / product flow.

this tool probably does not rise to the level of a DMAIC project. This is one of those just-do-it things. Decide the maximum amount wanted of something, create a space to hold it, and don't let anyone add more than the space can hold.

TRANSPORTATION (AND MOTION)

Transportation and motion are two sides of the same waste coin and are often solved in a comparable way. This waste all comes down to flow. Many plants are not designed to minimize flow; often, reducing the overall footprint is the main objective of the original architect. As a result, processes are placed where they fit without regard to relationship to supplies, tools, or other processes. This can add costs to the system and increase overall processing time. What can one do?

Often, a major redesign of the production flow would require a large capital investment. It might indeed be worth the investment, but the effort is outside of the DMAIC realm. If you are fortunate enough to be able to move machines around, great, start scribbling out those spaghetti diagrams and get to it!

However, there can still be opportunities to reduce these wastes by looking at the supporting processes like maintenance, sampling, testing, etc. Figuring out what excess movement is required to perform these tasks is the perfect assignment for a CI team and requires minimal training.

Table 4 illustrates a mini path for motion reduction.

Table 4 Mini-path for motion reduction.

		Reducing Motion	
Team Name:			
	Step	**Objectives/Key Activities**	**Done?**
D	Team Information	Organize the team	
		Choose team leader, facilitator, and coach	
		Choose target process area for improvement	
		Develop communication plan	
M	Current State	Create a map of current motion	
		Develop a map of target process area	
		Conduct observation events using spaghetti diagrams	
A	Find Waste	Find waste in map	
		Analyze map for unnessary motion	
		Determine reasons for necessary motion	
I	Reduce Waste	Find ways to reduce motion	
		Look for opportunities to relocate materials and supplies	
		Look for opportunities to combine activities to reduce trips	
		Look for opporties to eliminate activities	
		Create new spaghetti diagram showing improvements	
C	Capture Lessons	Reapply lessons and document changes	
		Reapply changes to similar process areas	
		Modify procedures to capture changes	
		Celebrate team's success	

WAITING

The next waste is waiting, or idle time. We can think about the idle time of machines or the idle time of people—not always the same thing.

MACHINE IDLE TIME

The only machine idle time we should care about is the idle time in our process bottleneck. Efforts to reduce idle time away from the bottleneck can be driven by poor accounting practices that measure and try to maximize the efficiency of every machine. This can lead to inventory waste as discussed earlier. Idle time away from the bottleneck is not a waste.

Some people advocate "line balancing" as the ideal situation, wherein all steps in a process have similar capacity thereby eliminating idle time for any step. I believe this thinking is flawed because it creates a situation where any hiccup in any step can affect the overall throughput of the process. Instead, I advocate a "V-shaped" capacity strategy that pushes into a designed bottleneck and pulls away from it (Figure 20).

Ideally, the most reliable step in your process should be the bottleneck and this should define the capacity of the process. All other steps should have excess capacity. The amount of excess capacity needed depends on the length and frequency of downtime in each step and the amount of buffering between steps. (The reducing failures path goes into this analysis in detail.)

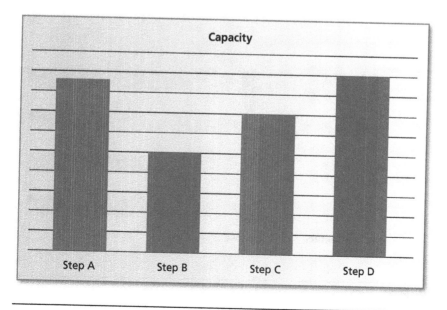

Figure 20 V-shaped capacity planning.

One of the key drivers of downtime length is time-to-repair. If there is idle time at the bottleneck due to downtime, we can try to improve by reducing time-to-repair.

Time-to-repair is made up of four stages (Figure 21):

- Detection
- Diagnosis
- Preparation
- Repair

Reducing the time of any of the stages will reduce the overall time-to-repair. Let's look at each stage.

Detection is about knowing quickly when you have a problem. Sometimes it is obvious when a process stops, but not always. If a step in the process is unattended or away from the main action, it might take a while for the impact of its downtime to be felt. Setting up indicators for every step that can stop the process is an effective way to minimize detection time.

Diagnosis is the time needed to figure out what went wrong. Sometimes this is not easy. Some machines are smart and give codes to help, but even then it's necessary to determine the root cause. A CI team can reduce diagnostic time by creating guides and checklists for the most common or expensive failures, by adding sensors or indicators, and through training. The goal is to allow anyone to perform the diagnosis, not just an expert who always seems to be unavailable just when needed.

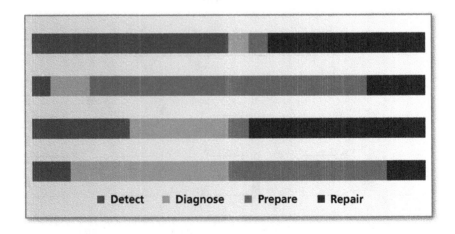

Figure 21 Various examples of time-to-repair stages.

Preparation is the time needed to gather materials, parts, and tools needed to perform a repair. The time required for this stage depends on many of the basic plant systems—the tool room, spare parts strategy, and work orders. Rethinking these systems to minimize repair preparation time can have a significant impact on time-to-repair. A CI team could develop a list of the more common repairs and have everything necessary at hand right where needed.

Repair is the time needed to complete the repair and get the machine back into operation. This stage includes any set-up, adjustments, and QC needed. Standard procedures and training are key to minimizing this time. A team might find that some people are much faster than others at a particular repair and should ask why. Some repairs require lengthy adjustments to achieve quality targets and a team could study how to get to target easier and faster. Also, some elements of SMED can be applied to common repairs to improve access, reduce tools needed, and eliminate adjustments.

Autonomous Maintenance

One of the best tools for reducing time-to-repair comes from the TPM toolbox—autonomous maintenance (AM). The basic concept of AM is to increase the ability of those operating equipment to keep it running. In some operations, when a machine stops the operator calls someone from the maintenance team and then heads out for a smoke break. Through AM, operators learn how to handle minor stops and adjustments themselves and thereby reduce, or even eliminate, time-to-repair. It is a powerful approach.

Implementing full-blown autonomous maintenance usually requires a huge culture change and is beyond the scope and abilities of any DMAIC team; however, as we do in all the paths, we can borrow certain ideas and tools. We don't have to do a full implementation of AM to see some of the benefits.

Let's look at the first few steps in a typical autonomous maintenance implementation:

- Clean—Let's make it easy to see if there is a problem somewhere.

- Eliminate deterioration sources—Let's reduce the need for recleaning.

- Implement clean-inspect-lubricate—Let's use cleaning time to inspect for problems and perform minor preventive maintenance tasks such as adding grease or oil.

- Learn to adjust—Let's create targets for things that can be adjusted and reaction plans to implement when things go wrong with product quality or machine performance.

- Correct minor abnormalities—Let's teach basic mechanical skills and only call the maintenance team when there is a major issue.

A DMAIC team could handle any or all these steps and have a significant impact on downtime. These improvement tools can and should be used by anyone who needs them. Don't wait for someone to "stand up" the AM pillar in a major TPM initiative.

Putting this all together, Table 5 illustrates a mini path for reducing time-to-repair.

Table 5 A mini-path to time-to-repair.

		Reducing Time-to-Repair	
Team Name:			
Step		**Objectives/Key Activities**	**Done?**
D	Team Information	Organize the team	
		Choose team leader, facilitator, and coach	
		Choose repair process for improvement	
		Develop communication plan	
M	Current State	Determine distribution of repair times	
		Collect data on time to complete repair	
		Create distribution of repair times	
A	Analyze	Determine time for each stage of repair	
		Look at distribution for special causes and calculate mean time-to-repair	
		Observe repairs and determine time for each stage	
I	Reduce Time	Find ways to reduce time in each stage	
		Look for opportunities to improve Detection	
		Look for opportunities to improve Diagnosis	
		Look for opportunties to improve Preparation	
		Look for opportunties to improve Repair	
C	Standardize	Lock in improvements	
		Implement training for new procedures	
		Put metric in place to monitor future repair times	
		Celebrate team's success	

PEOPLE IDLE TIME

People idle time is just what it sounds like—people hanging around waiting for something to do. Is this a bad thing? Of course, the answer is "it depends." If these people are involved in a process bottleneck, their idle time could directly correlate to lost throughput and we should be very concerned and work to reduce the reasons for loss.

But, what if their job is to fix a highly reliable process and their services are only needed occasionally but immediately? There is not much to do when things are running smoothly. Reminds me of the old Maytag repairman commercial—sometimes not being needed is a good thing!

In my view, we are way too quick to cut heads these days in order to eliminate this "waste." Instead we should look to engage the minds attached to these people during their "idle" time. Thinking is not non-value added! In fact, I think we don't allow our people enough thinking time. This is the perfect time to do the important but not urgent stuff. The cost benefit of eliminating a head can be far out-weighed by the benefit of engaging our "idle" resources in CI.

The ideas in this book may make it easier to do this engaging. If continuous improvement seems like a big, complicated thing that requires weeks of training and months of effort, then one can understand the hesitancy to commit to it. But if we split it into bite-size chunks that you can learn in minutes and implement in hours, then it becomes the perfect way to consume small amounts of idle time, improve something and increase people's value and self-worth. Wow, all that just from changing the way we approach CI.

OVER PROCESSING

Over processing is another important waste but one that a CI team cannot often reduce. Let's look at few scenarios of over processing to illustrate:

- Product/packaging design—This is the classic example of over processing waste and can be found in the over-design of packaging or in features of the product itself. Many hands are usually involved in these kinds of decisions and ideally the decisions are made based on a detailed understanding of customer requirements gained through quality function deployment (QFD) or some similar tool (Figure 22). I have found that QFD is best done in

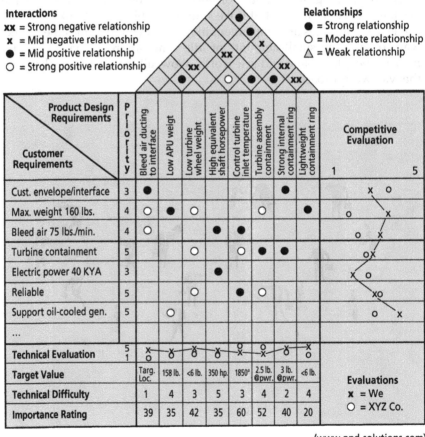

(www.npd-solutions.com)

Figure 22 Example of QFD.

a Kaizen event rather than as a DMAIC and that outside experts in the tool can be very useful. Here is a good reference on QFD: ASQ/ANSI/ISO 16355-1:2015: Application of statistical and related methods to new technology and product development process — Part 1: General principles and perspectives of Quality Function Deployment (QFD).

The outcome of the QFD should dictate the features of both product and packaging that the customers value. Anything in excess should be eliminated.

- Too-tight tolerances – This is another classic example of over processing. Specifications should be sacrosanct, but they should also reflect true fit-for-use limits. Arbitrarily tight specifications—those beyond customer requirements—do nothing but cause problems and lead to waste.

  - The first problem comes in setup when natural variability in a process makes it difficult to qualify the process for ongoing production. I've seen cases where a characteristic is in-spec or out-of-spec based on chance alone. The poor people on the line had to take and measure samples until they just happened to get an OK result. The measurement took quite some time and they could have achieved the same result in less time by rolling some dice or flipping a coin.

  - The second problem shows up in the over-reaction to ongoing results. An out-of-spec reading requires action in most QC systems. It's easy to see that if wider specs are acceptable, then reactions and reaction time would be reduced. The situation is even worse when trying to use SPC and the calculated control limits are outside the spec limits. Oh boy! We should all know that the process doesn't care about spec limits and that the control limits describe the best that process can currently do, but the effort required to convince QA and maybe even the auditing customer of this can be huge (and often futile.) How does one teach the underlying principles of SPC amid an audit? And all because some engineer, at some long-past time, pulled the "limits" out of thin air and now you're stuck with them.

So, what to do? Can a DMAIC team fix this? Maybe.

The first step is to eliminate "internal" specs that are narrower than actual customer specs. Created with good intentions, these actually do more harm than good. A better way is to continually drive capability improvement based on customer specs. This will automatically focus efforts on the at-risk characteristics and force understanding of natural variability.

Next, make customer specs as wide as possible. Determining fit-for-use specifications requires some investigation and the cooperation of the customer (Table 6). The basic idea is to create product at the edges of the spec range and test for "fitness." Blind testing is best in order to avoid any preconceived biases. A team might be able to drive this type of effort depending on the complexity of the effort.

Ideally, this exercise will give the widest specifications. If you're still not good enough or are stuck with the specs you have, I would suggest using the Reduce Variability path.

Visual Standards

Over processing can also involve waste from rejects due to lack of inspection standards for visual quality attributes—things such as color, size, clarity, roundness, surface quality, and so on. We all know one inspector who is more critical than the others and finds more "defects." Maybe she is too picky. Or, maybe she is correct and everyone else lets things pass, but that's not over processing and we put customers at risk by letting true defects get through. Either way, it's not a good situation.

The best way to solve this situation is to establish visual standards. The most basic visual standard illustrates a target. A better visual standard illustrates both a target and what high and low defective looks like. The best visual standards have a five-point scale—low bad, low but ok, target, high but ok, high bad (Figure 23).

Table 6 Checklist for setting fit-for-use specifications.

Setting Fit-For-Use Specifications		
Team Name:		
Step	Objectives/Key Activities	Done?
D Team Information	Organize the team	
	Choose team leader, facilitator, and coach	
	Identify critical customers and include on team	
M Current State	Establish current variabiity	
	Determine critical characteristics	
	Collect samples at various levels for each characteristic	
A Analyze	Determine specifications	
	Evaluate acceptability of extreme samples with customer	
	Determine fit-for-use limits for each characteristic	
I Reduce Time	Determine capability to meet specifications	
	Conduct trials to determine settings that meet specs	
	Calculate capability to meet specs	
	Initiate improvement activity if capability is low	
C Standardize	Lock in improvements	
	Develop/revise standards to match specs	
	Train people on new standards	
	Confirm acceptabiity with customers	

| Too light | OK light | OK | OK dark | Too dark |

Figure 23 An example of the best visual standard.

This will usually eliminate most of the differences between inspectors and insure no defects get to the customer. And it's the perfect thing for an improvement team to do one afternoon!

Manufacturing Routes

Another cause of over processing waste is using more costly processes than are needed, like using an expensive laser for cutting something simple or a CNC machine when dimensional tolerances are not critical. If you have a choice of manufacturing routes to produce something, you can reduce this waste by using the optimal or lowest-cost route. This is critical if it allows you to relieve a bottleneck process by off-loading to a good-enough alternative process. This is typically not a task for a CI team.

DEFECTS

This waste has its very own path through the DMAIC. See the next section.

* * *

Reducing Defects Path

A wise man once said, "Quality *begins* in the absence of defects." In other words, we can't even begin to talk about "six sigma" quality until we get rid of any defects. For this book, a *defect* is defined as any unwanted attribute or characteristic. It is something that shouldn't be there—dents, scratches, holes, smears, typos, and so on. The target level for defects is zero! Of course, a characteristic that is out-of-specification can be considered a defect, but that type of problem is dealt with in the section on reducing variability.

This type of problem is what the classic PDCA cycle or team problem-solving methods were meant to address, and they work great. Somehow, this basic method has gotten lost in the world of Lean Six Sigma. Sure, defects are one of the seven wastes, but the "how" of defect reduction is skimmed over in a lot of belt training. Yes, all the tools are there. And yes, concepts such as "root cause" and "biggest hitter" are covered, but the simple method that served many of us so well in our early years is lost in the web of Lean Six Sigma green/black belt training.

Whatever happened to basic problem-solving?

Let's bring it back. It's powerful, it's simple, and it can be done by anybody with a few hours of training. The ideas and tools are considered easy and are covered in countless (forgotten?) books. I'll lay out the methodology that I grew up with below, but you probably have a similar methodology somewhere in the company archives. Dust it off and start using it!

One point I'll make here is that there is a continuum of methods for problem-solving that range from the simple to the more involved, as illustrated in Figure 24.

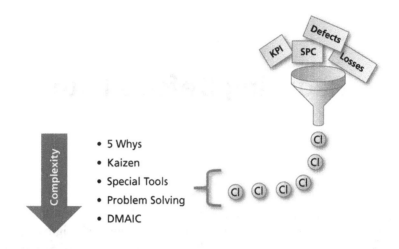

Figure 24 Various problem-solving methodologies.

All of these methods should be in active use in some form throughout the organization. If we can drive out the mystery, complications, and fear of CI tools, we can get people to apply them routinely as a habit. That's when the magic of CI starts to happen. That's when its full potential will be unleashed!

METHODOLOGY

There are lots of models out there for defect reduction that work well (Red Thread, Is/Is Not, PDCA), but here is one I like. It's not necessary to have a Green belt, or a belt of any color, to use the simple method involving these steps:

1. Reason for improvement

2. Current situation

3. Cause analysis

4. Solutions/countermeasures

5. Results

6. Standardization

7. Future plans

STEP DETAILS

1. Reason for Improvement

In this step the team will identify why this problem is important. Ideally, management will determine why the problem is worthy of a CI effort in the first place! The team can look at customer data, choose an indicator to track improvement, determine how much improvement is needed, and write a clear statement of the problem.

Reduce the number of jams at the infeed lift conveyor by 50% in two months.

2. Current Situation

Step 2 is to describe what is currently happening and define the gap between current and target performance levels. You will collect existing data and summarize it in simple line graphs to show the problem, create a flow chart of the process, and refine the problem statement if necessary to make the scope of the team effort clear (Figure 25).

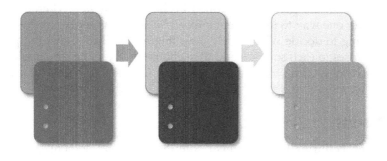

Figure 25 Illustration of a flow.

3. Analysis

In step 3, data is collected to find the causes of the problem. This involves brainstorming, creating fishbone diagrams, observing the process, and using checklists. A key tool in this step is the Pareto chart, which shows the major contributors to the problem (Figure 26). The team should stay in the analysis step until they have confirmed identification of root cause. Leaving the is step too early is a common error and leads to the problem returning rather than being solved.

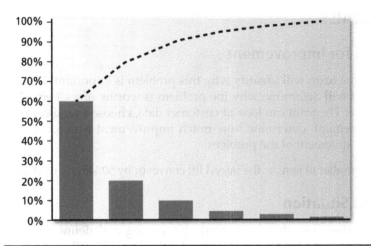

Figure 26 A Pareto chart indicating causes.

4. Solutions

Sometimes called countermeasures, solutions are the proposed fixes to the root causes of the problem identified in the previous step. There may be more than one way to implement a fix and a solution matrix is a great tool for helping to decide which one is best (Figure 27). To use, list the pluses and minuses to each solution and then choose the best one. You could also rate each solution on impact and difficulty. Choose the high impact, low difficulty options, and avoid the low impact, high difficulty ones.

5. Results

This step confirms that whatever solutions were implemented actually worked. The indicator chosen in the first step should clearly show the impact (Figure 28). Depending on the process and the nature of the defect, it can sometimes take a while for the results to come in.

Figure 27 A solution matrix.

6. Standardization

Standardization is the key to locking in improvement, preventing back-sliding, and expanding identified solutions to other similar areas or processes (Figure 29). This step usually involves training and updating of standards and procedures.

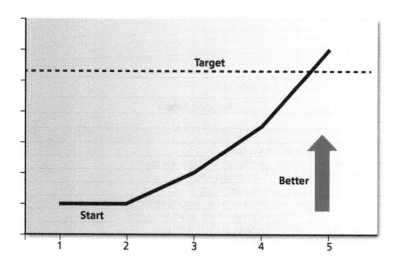

Figure 28 Results indicator.

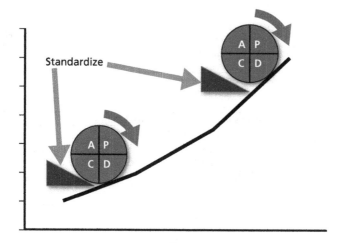

Figure 29 Standardization of solutions.

7. Future Plans

The final step is to determine what else should be done with this problem and to evaluate the effectiveness of the team (Table 7). Was the objective of the team met entirely or just partially? What follow-up is recommended? How did the team leader, facilitator, and coach perform? What could be done better? This important step, which is often missed, can lead to more effective CI systems.

CHECKLIST

Table 7   Checklist for reducing defects.

		Reducing Defects	
Team Name:			
	Step	**Objectives/Key Activities**	**Done?**
D	Team Information	Organize the team	
		Choose team leader, facilitator, and coach	
		Establish team ground rules	
		Determine location for storyboard	
	Reason For Improvement	Identify the reason for working on the problem	
		Articulate customer needs (internal/external)	
		Verify importance of effort (with data)	
		Select indicator to track performance	
		Determine ideal level of indicator	
		Write clear problem statement	
M	Current Situation	Determine current levels and improvement targets	
		Create flowchart of process	
		Collect all existing data on indicator	
		Identify current performance gap	
		Determine improvement goal for this effort	
		Create chart of indicator	
A	Analysis	Identify and verify the root cause(s) of the problem	
		Brainstorm possible causes	
		Collect data on possible causes	
		Determine actual root causes	
		Verify root causes using data	
I	Counter-measures	Implement solutions that correct root causes	
		Develop and evaluate potential solutions	
		Develop action plan to implement solutions	
		Get management approval for action plan	
		Implement solutions according to action plan	
	Results	Confirm that solutions were effective	
		Check for improvement of indicator	
		Compare results to targets	
		Analyze reasons for success / failure	
		Continue to implement other solutions if needed	

(continued)

Table 7   Checklist for reducing defects *(continued)*.

Reducing Defects		
Team Name:		
Step	**Objectives/Key Activities**	**Done?**
C Standard-ization	Standarize procedures to prevent reoccurance	
	Create/update procedures to capture effective countermeasures	
	Train affected employees on procedures	
	Replicate solutions to other similar areas	
	Set up indicator for regular monitoring to maintain gains	
Future Plans	Plan future action needed and celebrate success	
	Recommend future actions	
	Conduct evaluation of team effectiveness	
	Plan celebration of team's accomplishments	

What Comes Next?
How Can You Do This?

If you've made it this far in the book, I hope you're convinced of the wisdom of this new approach and I hope you're ready to go. If you skipped to this chapter because you're a doer (or I told you to in the beginning), you won't be disappointed. This is where the doing happens. And if there is one thing this book is about, it's about doing! But first, allow me a moment to set the table before we start eating.

LOOSEN THE BELTS

In my view, the whole martial arts "belt" construct so common in the CI world these days is flawed. There are no standards and a belt doesn't indicate what skills people have or what they can do.

If you want to earn a belt in the martial arts, you must learn more than kicks, punches, and throws. You must master *katas*. Katas combine the individual moves into specific routines that demonstrate how the moves work together to accomplish an objective—disarm an attacker, defend against multiple attackers, and so on. Each belt level has its own katas that build on previous ones. You must demonstrate each kata to expert judges who verify your knowledge. By the time you reach black belt you have mastered and demonstrated many katas of varying complexity. For example, in Shotokan karate there are 26 katas ranging from the most basic (Heian Shodan, which has 21 moves) up to the advanced Gojushiho Dai (which has 67 moves). *(www.shotokankaratecalgary.com)*

Contrast this with how people earn Lean Six Sigma belts. In the "certification" programs I've come across, belt candidates go through one to three weeks of training in which they "learn" CI tools along with theory and maybe some people skills. Then they "demonstrate" their skills with a project or two. There is no telling how much of the universe of LSS methods the chosen projects cover. Some programs require people use tools that make no sense just so they can "practice." There is no way to know what that person is capable of doing. That's why you'll get "I'm more of a lean guy" when you ask a certified "Black Belt" about his experience. How is this useful?

QUALITY KATAS

What if, instead, we came up with a list of "quality katas" and certified people to those? What if we figured out what things we need people to do and then teach them to do those things? Below are a few examples of the suggested quality katas for each of the paths. Note that they are not tools but actions. They accomplish a specific thing.

Reduce Variability

- Create a process map
- Determine the natural variability of a process
- Evaluate a continuous measurement system
- Evaluate an attribute measurement system
- Deploy a control chart
- Create a special-cause reaction tree
- Conduct a fit-for-use specification study

Reduce Failures

- Create a process map
- Improve MTBF
- Reduce MTTR
- Implement predictive tools
- Perform AU loss analysis
- Reduce changeover duration
- Find the effective bottleneck of a process
- Identify and mitigate risk of failure modes

Reduce Waste

- Conduct a sort event
- Implement a Kanban
- Remove deterioration sources
- Implement centerlining in a process
- Conduct an SMED event

Reduce Defects

- Perform a Pareto analysis
- Compare two samples
- Compare many samples
- Eliminate potential mistakes
- Conduct a structured brainstorming session

There are many more. You may even have some unique to your business. Find them.

If we insist on continuing the martial arts analogy, we could change the criteria for belts to something like the number of quality katas a person can do. Learn a few and you're a green belt. Learn all of them and you're a black belt. Learn to teach the quality katas and you're a master black belt. That way, you know what you're getting when someone says they are a certain belt.

But I don't think we need belts. I think belts do more for egos and resumes than they do for furthering our continuous improvement efforts. Maybe we should go with ribbons instead, or kata badges like the Boy Scouts? I love the visual of person's office or personal webpage decorated with badges. We would know what people have accomplished and not what classes they have attended. It would be easy then to assemble a team of people with the right combination of skills for a particular challenge.

Many businesses need only some of the quality katas. Very few need them all. Why not focus on the ones that are critical for your business? Let's apply a little non-value-added (NVA) elimination to our CI training! That's what this book is all about and that's what is meant by "splitting the DMAIC."

Let's split CI into quality katas, train the katas, and combine them into paths. Then we'll have people who can actually do the things we need done. We'll have lots of people who are experts at one or two things rather than a few people who are amateurs at everything. In fact, you probably already have people in your organization who have mastered some of the katas. This approach lets you use what those people have already accomplished—the weeks/months/years of training are not wasted! We just recognize the limits of the previous training and give credit to people only for things actually learned and demonstrated.

You in? Great, let's do this.

THE DOING

Here are some steps you could follow to implement this thinking:

1. Identify the paths that matter to your business. (You can use the ones in this book!)

2. Determine the katas on the paths. (Or use the steps I've outlined.)

3. Assess current skills to deliver katas on these paths.

4. Develop or redefine training on the critical paths and katas.

5. Create a list of specific things that must be improved.

6. Charter improvement efforts on the chosen opportunities and use the right path.

Let's look a little deeper into each of these steps.

1. Identify the paths that matter to your business.

The first and most critical thing to recognize is what type of business you are in and what paths you need. What is the nature of your operation?

- High speed/low speed
- Continuous/batch
- Automated/manual
- Assembly/forming
- Tight specs/loose specs
- High changeover/long runs

Combine these attributes into the key drivers for business improvement. If you are high speed, continuous operation and are constrained by capacity, then consider making use of the Reducing Failures path to increase throughput. If you have demanding customers with tight specs and low yields, the Reducing Variability path could be the most impactful by allowing you to improve quality and increase yields. Almost all operations find a need for the Reducing Defects path and the Reducing Waste path to lower costs. It's also possible that your needs will change over time. The limits on your business will likely change as you improve.

2. Determine the katas on the paths.

OK, this is not easy. It's one of the reasons why I think companies struggle with CI. It's hard to put the tools together in the right combination to be successful at improvement. Success often depends on the strength of the person leading the effort and really good people are hard to come by. I suggest you start out just using the paths as I've laid them out here. They work!

If you happen to have the right expertise in your organization, put it to use to customize a path. Tweak what you see here or create a unique mini-path. The trick is to make the path easy to follow. Break it into simple katas and train your folks on them. You'll be amazed at the results you can get when you give your people a path that intuitively makes sense to them, that fits the problems they have, and that they can understand. They will love you for it.

3. Assess current skills to deliver katas on these paths.

Be honest. Have you put your best people into CI roles? If so, great! These people should be excited to focus on the critical paths and perhaps learn new skills. If not, then let's take a step back and assess where we are. The good news is that this new approach doesn't rely on the skills of any individual CI person for success. Everyone becomes a CI person because it's no longer this mysterious, complicated mess. The katas and paths are simple and cookbook. The barriers to CI entry are gone.

However, you still need someone to figure this out. You need at least one person who is skilled enough to understand all the paths and who knows what is needed and when. You need someone who can look ahead and plan the overall journey.

You can also add the paths (or at least the katas) to everyone's development plan and make them mandatory for promotion into certain positions. I call this the infiltration strategy; if you only promote people with CI skills, then eventually everyone in leadership has them. You no longer need a large, central CI group. You just need someone who can point the way to the next level of maturity.

Find, or rent, a good leader for continuous improvement and pay this person well. (I'm available!)

4. Develop or redefine training on the critical paths and katas.

How to approach training is probably the major decision that most organizations will make. We must get away from the weeks-long "belt" training. We need JIT training. We need agile training. (I promised my editor that I would fit "agile" in somewhere, since that is the latest buzzword.) Above all, we need simple training that anyone can understand without a degree in statistics or human behavior. We do not need people to know the underlying theory of a CI method to be successful. People do not need to know how the internal combustion engine works to drive a car, they just need basic instructions and a map. It's the same with almost all of CI if you define the paths—create the map—ahead of time.

Remember, we are not trying to create a small group of people with elite skills. We don't need roving bands of experts. We are trying to create an army of people with just enough skills. The burden is on us to break the complicated into the simple.

Let's break the Lean Six Sigma training we already have into paths. Or, better yet, just start from scratch if the design of your current training does not meet the new intent. I learned a long time ago that designing good training materials is not easy and that how you go about it is determined by the level of knowledge you wish to impart. For example, getting people to each of the levels below requires differing amounts of effort:

- Be familiar with a concept.
- Be able to apply concept in same way as taught.
- Be able to explain concept to someone else.
- Be able to apply concept in a new way.
- Be able to train others in use of concept.

What is the aim of your training? Too often training only gets to the first level—we "cover" the material—as if a vocabulary lesson is sufficient teaching. Or else we go the other way and try to make people college professors in a particular subject when they only need to be at the second level.

Let's also find a way to offer the training of specific skills in a just-in-time manner. Need to do an R&R? Here's a two-hour class. Need to slice and dice data to find the "big-hitters"? Here's one hour on the Pareto principle. Trying to reduce motion? Let's show you how to do a spaghetti diagram. The point is to get away from teaching tools and start teaching specific skills:

- Visualize variability with a histogram.
- Show relationships with a scatter plot.
- Determine if two means are different.
- Determine probability of a certain outcome.
- Do a short-term capability study.
- Create a Gantt chart.
- Determine losses at the bottleneck.
- Etc.

We can think about all the skills someone in a particular position might need and create a curriculum of classes around them. Classes can be grouped in various ways to meet different needs and to make training more efficient. A great way to organize and track all this is with a skills matrix (Figure 30). A skills matrix can be organized by person or function

1 = Awareness 2 = Proficient 3 = Expert	Specialist / Sr. Specialist	Scientist / Sr. Scientist	Engineer / Sr. Engineer	Research Principal / Sr. Res. Prin.	Manager / Sr. Manager	Research Fellow / Sr. Res. Fellow	Director / Sr. Director	Distinguished Research Fellow	Vice President	Senior Vice President	Designs Experiments/ Trials	Analyzes Experimental Data	Manages Internal / External Information	Leads Program	Leads Projects	Leads Teams	Conducts Scale Up Studies	Runs Plant Trials
Basic Statistics																		
Experiments																		
Hypothesis Testing																		
Measurement Analysis																		
Problem Solving																		
Capability Analysis																		
Process Control																		
Risk Management																		
FMEA																		
Reliability																		
5S																		

Figure 30   Skills matrix.

or path and used to determine who needs what skills and to identify the gaps.

You might notice in the example that there is something called a skill level. This is the target level we talked about earlier and it's a way to recognize that not everyone needs the same level of a skill. Some need to be expert in a particular skill while others just need to be familiar with the concept or even just the vocabulary.

Be careful, though. The step from the first level to the second level is a big one. I have found that most people cannot get to level two by reading from slides—no matter the PowerPoint skills of the creator. There must also be muscle memory. There must also be *doing*. So, lets move our training to the floor and make it interactive and hands-on.

Let's get visual, visual. (Apologies to Olivia Newton-John.)

Everyone agrees that a picture is worth a thousand words, right? Well, we can be more effective in our training by using the same thinking we put into visual standards and work instructions. These work better than written instruction because we can convey so much more information on a page with diagrams, examples, and pictures than we can with words.

It's the same with training. We need to be creative in the same way. Especially if someone is only going after level two—just reapply as taught. Skip all the theory, history, what-if scenarios, and unlikely variations and focus on doing.

Let's turn the katas into simple, visual work instructions and the paths into simple, repeatable checklists. Then try to get the training for each down to an hour or less. This truly opens up an agile approach to training.

5. Create a list of specific things that must be improved.

I cover team chartering in detail below, but it's worth repeating here. People should not choose their own improvement projects! Each facility should develop and maintain a list of the things they would improve if they only had the resources. It goes without saying that this list should be linked to critical business needs of the facility. If this list doesn't exist or is hard to come up with, then we have a problem with KPIs and objectives rather than CI.

A disconnect between CI projects and the business needs is, I think, one of the main reasons improvement efforts fizzle. There just isn't the interest or energy to finish. When the connection is there, the support and the energy are there, too.

The path approach also makes it easier to identify projects. It is easier to think about which defect to reduce or where lower variability would help than it is to think about a "good" LSS project where all the tools can be used.

The other thing this path approach does is to reduce the size of projects and the time to complete. Instead of nine- to twelve-month projects that seem to go on forever, many paths are fast, hard-hitting efforts that last only days or weeks and quickly accomplish something! Imagine needing a monthly celebration to recognize all the wins that keep coming. Now that's unleashing the power of CI.

6. Implement improvement efforts on the chosen paths.

In one of my previous companies, we made a study of why some locations were very effective with CI teams and others were just ok. We found that the factors related to team effectiveness can be grouped into five categories:

- Management support
- Priorities and resources
- Training and skills
- Recognition and motivation
- Communication and teamwork

Chartering is intertwined in most of these factors. Let's have a look at chartering and other things that contribute to these factors.

CHARTERING

What's one of the first things many organizations ask their budding belts or CI team leaders to do? Create a charter! They are expected to pick a problem, come up with an objective (must be SMART!), form a team, choose a metric, and justify the expected savings. Then, they must get "consensus" that the project fits into everyone's priorities and document any resistance with something called a "shareholder analysis." And just for good measure, the projected savings must be above some arbitrary number or it doesn't count. Wow! All this before the first week of Green Belt training is over. It's no wonder people are intimidated. It's no wonder there are lots of safe and silly projects. It's no wonder that being selected for CI feels like you lost the *Hunger Games* lottery!

This is not to say that charters aren't important; they are critical. But in my experience they should be given to CI teams and not developed by them.

A good chartering process is linked to a location's strategic plan and based on gaps in key metrics. A location's management team should always have a list of the top four to six things they want to work on next. These things come from analysis—updated weekly, monthly, continuously—of performance data against targets. Struggling with efficiency of a particular product? Too much scrap from a certain process? Is there a chronic customer complaint? Want to improve the margin on a critical segment?

These are the types of objectives that should feed the CI process.

In this way, the objectives of CI teams are automatically linked to the right priorities. The CI teams know they are working on something important and can see the clear connection to performance. Others give their full support because they also know the importance of the missions. None of the projects are silly. None need a "shareholder" analysis—the shareholders gave the charter!

There are two types or sizes of projects to consider. There are those where a big step change is needed and those where small improvements will do. We should aim for a few of the first and a whole bunch of the second. Forget the silly size requirements for "certification" and let's start taking any improvement. In fact, many argue it's the small incremental improvements that lead to excellence and a real culture of CI (Jeffrey K. Liker, James K. Franz. 2011. *Toyota Way to Continuous Improvement*. The McGraw-Hill Companies, Inc.) Let's get everyone in the organization engaged in CI projects no matter how small. There will end up being a few big ones in there (Figure 31).

In addition to the objective, one of the keys things a charter should give is the path through the DMAIC. The management team should decide which path is appropriate for the objective they have chosen. Imagine the head start a team would have if it were given its specific objective and a recommended route to accomplish that objective. Many more teams would be successful if they followed this approach.

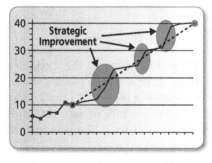 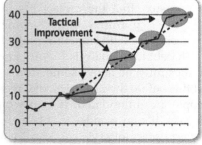

Figure 31   Strategic vs. tactical improvements.

In summary, a team chartering system is the process that ensures a team gets the best start possible and should include the following critical elements:

- The strategy the team is to follow
- Team goals
- How the goals link to plant priorities
- How long the team has to complete the goals (should be fast!)
- The leader and coach of the team
- Suggested team members
- An assessment of team member skills/training
- Pre-existing background information (lessons learned, current I/O matrix, etc.)
- Team kick off meeting

ROLES/COACHING

The next key element to a successful team-based CI program is wide ownership/involvement in the facility. We can accomplish this by establishing and filling some clear roles.

Process Owner

The owner of the team process is directly accountable for the success of all teams in the plant. The process owner is responsible for:

- Ensuring that all team systems are in place and functioning properly
- Selecting team goals that align to plant priorities
- Assigning coaches and team leaders
- Having a process for team participant selection
- Ensuring that teams have time to meet and perform follow-up assignments

Process Leader

The process leader is responsible for the creation and maintenance of team systems and for providing technical expertise to the teams in data analysis. These include:

- Team chartering
- Choosing proper team strategy

- Training
- Communication
- Team reviews
- Recognition

Coach

A coach is a member of management and is directly accountable for the success of a specific team. The coach is expected to know, at any given time, what step the team is on, what activities they are involved in, and what barriers they face. A team's coach should actively work to remove these barriers by communicating to the management team and securing additional resources for the team as appropriate. Coaches should interact with their teams at whatever frequency is required to achieve this.

Team Leader

The team leader is responsible for scheduling and conducting team meetings, keeping the team focused on the goals and following the strategy, following up on assignments, keeping the storyboard and other communications current, and coordinating all other team activities. Team leaders should have these skills:

- Meeting management
- Facilitation
- Training in the strategy the team is using

Team Member

A team member is responsible for using the methods and tools of the appropriate strategy to improve the process that has been assigned to the team. All team members should take responsibility for and contribute to the team's success. Team members should:

- Attend and participate in all team meetings
- Use good meeting management techniques
- Use data to make decisions
- Keep track of progress through the strategy
- Update the team's storyboard
- Follow through on commitments

TRAINING

The CI training system in the plant should be designed to provide the appropriate skills to the appropriate people at the appropriate time. The goal is that 100% of the people on teams should be properly trained in the strategy they are following and the tools they are using.

One of the mistakes I've seen many companies make is to "go big" on "belt" training. They spend weeks putting people through a series of classes and at the end people have a lot of knowledge but can't actually do anything. Let's change that. Let's train people to do specific things in a simple way, such as:

- Reduce a defect
- Reduce variability of a critical characteristic
- Reduce planned downtime using SMED
- Complete a 5S project
- Make a gauge stable and capable
- Reduce wasted motion

COMMUNICATION AND RECOGNITION

The purpose of team communication and recognition systems is to increase the awareness of team activities and results and to positively reinforce the team process.

The communication system should use as many ways to communicate as manageable. Some of the more effective methods are:

- Storyboards
- Plant video systems
- Newsletters
- Shift meetings

The recognition system should also use various forms as appropriate to the plant environment. Some effective methods are:

- Mentions of CI activity in key meetings
- Walls of fame
- Letters to home
- Individual recognition (shirts, plaques, etc.)
- Newsletters
- Plant-wide celebrations

It's also important to somehow recognize the vital role of the employees not on formal CI teams. They often enable CI teams by covering for meetings, collecting special data, and helping in other ways.

REVIEWS

There should be a formal system for reviewing the progress and results of teams. The system should include various levels and frequencies of informal and formal reviews. At a minimum, the performance of every team should be formally reviewed by the management team once every quarter. New teams may require more frequent review. The formal reviews should ask whether the teams are:

- Focused on their mission
- Following the strategy
- Measuring success
- Using the proper tools
- Using the communication system
- In need of help

Records of all reviews should be maintained and used in subsequent reviews.

* * *

Digitalization

The digital era has begun to sweep over CI in a big way and the ideas in this book fit perfectly into this wave. Each path or even kata can be made accessible to anyone with a tablet or smart phone—i.e., to everyone. The checklist approach means that progress can be tracked instantly and help requested on demand. Collected data can be easily captured and even shared with other projects.

If you are looking at implementing some kind of pillar structure to manage your improvement efforts, this book could be the content for your entire CI pillar! It also points to the links in other pillars such as leadership, quality, people, standard work, and so on (Figure 32).

Adapting this strategy could also be the start to your digital transformation.

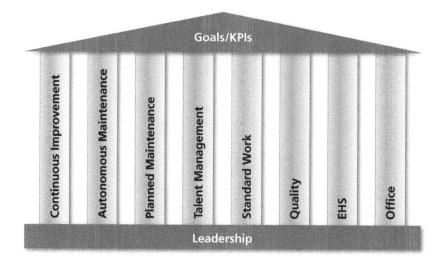

Figure 32   Goals/KPIs leadership pillar structure.

* * *

Summary and Conclusions

R ather than train your people on all the tools and methods they might possibly use some day, figure out what tools and methods your organization needs and train people on those.

Rather than a few elite "belts" who are supposed to know everything, create an army of specialists who are very good at one or two things and have them do these things repeatedly.

Rather than have people and teams flounder with project selection that includes the required list of tools, select projects for them based on your business drivers and use only the tools needed for that project.

Rather than vague "belt" designations where capability is unclear, let's name what a person is capable of accomplishing.

This is what is meant by the title of this book. You can unleash the true potential of your continuous improvement efforts by "Splitting the DMAIC." Start today.

***

References

A Brief History of Lean. Lean Enterprise Institute.

Autonomous Maintenance for Operators, edited by The Japan Institute of Plant Maintenance, CRC Press, 1997.

Barsalou, Matthew A. *Statistics for Six Sigma Black Belt*. ASQ, Milwaukee, WI. 2014.

Best, M. and D. Neuhauser. "Walter A Shewhart, 1924, and the Hawthorne Factory." *Quality & Safety in Health Care* 15.2 (2006): 142–143. PMC. Web. 19. Sept. 2018.

Faloran, J. "The evolution of Six Sigma." *Six Sigma Forum Magazine* (2003), Vol 2 Issue 4. http://asq.org/pub/sixsigma/past/vol2_issue4/folaron.html

Holweg, Matthias. "The genealogy of lean production." *Journal of Operations Management* 25.2 (2007): 420-437.

Learning Lean 5S: Quality Pocket of Knowledge (QPoK), ASQ, 2009.

Owens, Tracy. *Six Sigma Green Belt, Round 2*, ASQ, Milwaukee, WI. 2012.

Taylor, Frederick Winslow (1911) *The Principles of Scientific Management*, New York, NY, USA and London, UK: Harper & Brothers.

* * *

Index

Note: page numbers in *italics* indicate figures and tables.